# the
# change
# agent

"There is nothing permanent except change."

—Heraclitus


"There is nothing more difficult to take in hand, more perilous to conduct, or more uncertain in its success, than to take the lead in the introduction of a new order of things."

—Nicolo Machiavelli, *The Prince*, Chapter 6

# the change agent

## lyle e. schaller

**Abingdon Press**
Nashville

# THE CHANGE AGENT

ISBN 0-687-06042-7

Library of Congress Catalog Card Number: 77-185544

MANUFACTURED BY THE PARTHENON PRESS AT
NASHVILLE, TENNESSEE, UNITED STATES OF AMERICA

To Fred A. Clarenbach
David Fellman
Ivan A. Nestingen

# Contents

# Preface

Anyone seriously interested in planned social change would be well advised to recognize two facts of life. First, despite the claims of many, relatively little is known about how to achieve predictable change. Second, much of what is known will not work.

If taken seriously, and they are offered in complete seriousness, these two comments should discourage anyone from either reading or attempting to write a book on the process of planned change.

The alternatives, however, are even more clearly unacceptable. One alternative is to sit back and await what tomorrow may bring without any planning or preparation. Another is to plunge in blindly and attempt to initiate change without bothering to try to learn from the experiences of others or from the observations of social and behavioral scientists. That alternative has been chosen by an amazingly large number of persons, many of whom have become disillusioned, frustrated, or embittered by their experiences. It, too, is very unattractive.

A third alternative does exist, and it constitutes both the motivation for the writing of this book and the central theme of the contents. This is the assumption that each one of us can learn from the experiences of others, that an anticipatory style of leadership is the most effective style for an era when rapid social change is one of the few constants, and that despite his limitations, man can influence the future.

Consistent with the theme of this book is the notion that it may be helpful to the reader to be aware of some of the underlying assumption on which the contents are based, to be warned of a few of the more obvious biases and prejudices of the author, and to review the outline that was developed to present the central thesis of the book.

The first assumption on which this volume rests is that people can profit from the experiences, reflections, and insights of others. In one sense this book is an attempt to summarize what has been learned about the process of planned social change, to present this in a form that will be most useful to an agent of change, and to suggest, via the notes, opportunities for further reading on several aspects of the process.

A second assumption is that by action or by inaction every person does influence the future. Therefore, in one manner or another everyone is an agent of change. Some people are passive agents of change, others are negative agents of change, and an increasing number are becoming affirmative agents of change.

The third assumption is that violent revolution is not a viable alternative in the United States today. In a nation in which the central government can quickly control both the dominant forms of mass communication (radio, television, publishing, telephone, telegraph, and large meetings) and the armed forces, including the police, any serious attempt at rapid change through a violent overthrow of the government almost certainly would produce a repressive and totalitarian central government.

A fourth assumption is that the person who has a systematic approach to the future and a frame of reference for evaluating alternatives has a tremendous advantage over the person who functions without either. The purpose of this book is not to sell a particular system or frame of reference, but to encourage the reader to develop his own by illustrating the concept and suggesting alternatives.

A final basic assumption on which this volume rests is that God is at work in human history today, just as he has been in the past and will be tomorrow. The advocate of planned social change who does not believe this will find much in the past as well as in the present and the future that is incomprehensible.

Closely related to these basic assumptions are a series of biases and prejudices that have colored what is contained within these pages. While it obviously is impossible for anyone to make a complete list of his biases and prejudices, there are several that can be identified. The reader should be forewarned that I support the contemporary trend toward planned change despite the extravagant expectations that frequently accompany it, that I favor innovation as a generally superior form of planned change to either reform or revolution, that I believe the courts and legal structure offer one of the most productive routes for change, that I am in sympathy with those who favor accelerating the pace of change, that I am a firm believer in the sinful nature of man, and that I have a strong personal bias in favor of the enabler style of leadership for the change agent while still recognizing the essential role of the prophetic witness.

On the other hand, I hold a strong bias against those who either advocate or accept change by indecision or inaction, against the escalation of the level of violence in the United States, against the elitism articulated by Herbert Marcuse and his followers on the New Left, and against such self-defeating strategies as procrastination, anarchy, and revolution. I tend to be impatient with those who are constantly advocating the direct participation of all of the people in every decision that affects them just as I am impatient with those who insist on going through the laborious process of reinventing the wheel whenever a new issue is to be resolved. I find it easier to be tolerant of ignorance than of self-inflicted blindness.

For the reader who finds a road map a useful device in following an author's intentions, I should first identify the destination. The basic thesis of this book is that a systematic and anticipatory approach to planned social change is the most effective style for an agent of change. It should also be emphasized that the focus in this book is on planned social change in organizations and institutions. No effort has been made here to discuss personal growth or change in individuals.

The first chapter is an attempt to illustrate this thesis by three negative illustrations and to lift up the points at which a more systematic and forward-looking style could have prevented some of the disappointments that were encountered.

The nature of change is described in the second chapter with a special emphasis on two points. One is those characteristics of change which can be most helpful to the change agent. The other is the emphasis on innovation as an alternative to reform or revolution.

Perhaps the most critical skill for the anticipatory style of leadership among the advocates of change is to be able to understand the process of planned change. In the third chapter several definitions of the process are reviewed and a five-phase process is suggested as a model. This model has proved to be useful both in analyzing past events and in anticipating the future.

The individual who identifies himself as an agent of planned change may find it helpful to ask himself several questions about role, style, tactics, and his own biases. Several possibilities for these questions can be found in the fourth chapter. They are accompanied by suggestions that the person who is developing the enabler-anticipatory style may find useful.

One of the most widely discussed aspects of change is power, and this is the subject of the fifth chapter. This discussion is focused on the place of power as a factor in the social-change process, and an attempt is made to lift up some of the "either-or" choices confronting the change agent and to expose a few myths.

There are many points of conflict which are inherent in the process of intentional change, and these are identified in the sixth chapter along with several suggestions on how an anticipatory style of leadership can enhance the creativity and reduce the risks of polarization that often are by-products of conflict.

Unquestionably the most neglected dimension of planned social change comes under the label of what is now described as organizational development. Skill in this discipline is an essential part of the equipment of the effective change agent. The last chapter is an introduction to this subject.

In the writing of this book many debts and obligations were incurred, but they are too numerous to mention individually. One that must be mentioned, however, is the permission granted by Dr. Willis Bennett, editor of the *Review and Expositor*, to adapt portions of my article from the June, 1971, issue of that periodical for use in Chapter 6. The book is dedicated to three men who made major contributions to my life, my career, my thinking, and to the substance of this volume. For their contributions I am grateful.

Finally, lest anyone take too literally this brief on behalf of anticipatory leadership and planned social change, let him ponder the words ascribed to Judas in the rock-opera *Jesus Christ Superstar*, "I don't understand why you let the things you did get so out of hand, you'd have managed better if you'd had it planned."

# 1

## How to Cut Your Own Throat

I

"At our last staff meeting we agreed that we should recommend to the church council that every adult new member be encouraged to spend at least one year in a serious study group experience. If I understood our conversation correctly, we saw this as a means of making membership in this congregation a more meaningful experience for both the new member and for this church." With these comments the Reverend William Warren, senior minister of the prestigious nineteen-hundred-member downtown First Church, moved to take up the first item on the agenda at the weekly staff meeting.

"After thinking about this for a week, what do you suggest we do next?" he asked.

"I still think it's an excellent idea," responded Mrs. Benton, the director of Christian education. "However, I don't see this as another class in our church school. I think we need to present this in a broader frame of reference. I believe we should place more emphasis on this as a means of training and making available a group of potential new leaders for the church. I see this as a means of helping people grow and develop their own potential, of preparing new members for leadership responsibilities in this congregation, and of responding to what I believe is a real need to get some new blood in the lay leadership positions."

"I'm with Mrs. Benton! In three years we can turn this church completely around by a top-notch program for training and assimilating new members into the leadership of this church." This endorsement came from Jack Reynolds, the thirty-one-year-old assistant minister.

"Please don't misunderstand me," spoke up Dr. Carter, the sixty-six-year-old semiretired minister who served on a part-time basis as the minister of visitation for First Church. "I'm all in favor of more and better training for new members, whether they come in by letter of transfer or by confession of faith, but I believe our primary goal should be on helping these people become better Christians. If we do that we may not have to worry about turning this congregation around."

"I don't think there is any disagreement here," spoke up Mrs. Benton in an obvious effort to smooth over what threatened to be another clash between Mr. Reynolds and Dr. Carter. "This is clearly our goal, to help people become better Christians, and as they do this, to become the persons God intended them to be."

"A moment ago you asked what we should do next," she continued, this time addressing Dr. Warren. "I suggest that we ask Jack to take responsibility for planning and leading these groups. Dr. Warren gets acquainted with the new members in the membership training class before they join. If Jack could be delegated to lead these study groups for new members after they join, it would give him and the new members an opportunity to get better acquainted with one another."

"I'll support that proposal," added Dr. Carter. "Jack is more up-to-date than any of the rest of us on new ideas in theology and on contemporary thinking about the church, and he has the time to do a good job."

"Well, I guess you're it," commented Dr. Warren to Jack. "We have agreed this should be done and that you are the man to do it. To be perfectly frank with you, I am a bit envious. I would like to do this myself. I need the intellectual stimulation. I covet the chance to get better acquainted with the new members, and as chairman of the nominating committee, I would be in a good position to suggest people for office. However, between preaching, administrating, hospital calling, and getting ready for our $300,000 capital funds drive for remodeling the building, I simply don't have the time to take on any additional major long-term responsibilities."

Three months later the program was under way. The church council had approved it, and with a combination of eagerness and commitment Jack had given it a high priority on his own time. The practice at First Church was to receive new adult members nine times a year and the typical group included eight to twelve adults. These adults, together with the youth who joined by transfer or confirmation, totaled the 150 new members First Church required each year to offset the losses through deaths, transfers, and removals. Every three or four months Jack formed a new group from the twenty to thirty most recent new adult members. His enthusiastic approach may have been the primary reason that three out of every five new members not only agreed to join a group, but also stayed with it for the twelve monthly meetings that were a part of the covenant.

While there were many variations among the groups, the general theme that was proposed and followed in each one was "What Does It Mean to Be the Church in Today's World?" In addition to reading and discussion, each group took four field trips during the year to see firsthand examples of what progressive churches and church-sponsored agencies were doing in ministry.

The first group was so enthusiastic they continued for fifteen months before reluctantly disbanding. At this time a dozen members of that group were joined by a half-dozen persons from the second group and four from the third to form a new group or "cadre," as they called themselves. With Jack's enthusiastic leadership, with the apparent acquiescence of Dr. Warren, and with the quiet support of Mrs. Benton, this group met for study and discussion and also shared together in several lay training programs at retreat centers.

Three years after the program had been proposed, nine persons from this cadre had been elected to the twenty-member church council at First Church. Forty-one months after the first meeting of the first study group, a petition was presented at the church council meeting, signed by a bare majority of the members of the council, asking for Dr. Warren's resignation. After a stormy session that was not adjourned until 3 A.M., a compromise was reached. The petition was withdrawn, all references to it were deleted from the minutes, and oral commitments to resign were submitted by Dr. Warren, Mr. Reynolds, and Mrs. Benton.

What had happened?

In this congregation three progressive, change-oriented Christian leaders were forced to resign as they became victims, rather than facilitators, of the change process. To a degree, it can be argued that they were victims of circumstances, but to a far greater degree they were victims of their own acts. The unpleasant ending of this story was due largely to the ignoring or the flouting of several of the basic principles of planned change.

What happened?

First, as the members of these study groups examined the issue of what it means to be the church in today's world, they were unconsciously involving themselves in what is perhaps the most effective means of arousing a desire for change. This is the process of the self-identified discrepancy. As they discussed what the church should be in today's world, they could not help but become discontented with the discrepancy between this ideal and what they perceived to be reality at First Church.

Second, no constructive outlet was provided for this mounting discontent and no channel was opened for the new members to obtain a hearing for their grievances.

Third, in a normal, natural human response to a frustrating conflict situation they tended to drift away from the issues and to personify "the enemy," in this case the senior minister, Dr. Warren.

Fourth, by definition of the persons invited to join, the study-group process followed tended to prevent the creation of a common identity between the new members and the persons who had been members for a longer period of time and who constituted nearly all of the lay leadership in this large congregation.

Fifth in this process, as always and everywhere, education is alienating and no effort was made to reduce or to counter this process.

Sixth, as good Christians who were being encouraged to help bring in the Kingdom, these new members at First Church were allowed (encouraged?) to form a new congregation—the "cadre"—within the structure of First Church, but with no effective means of becoming assimilated into the decision-making process at First Church and without any effort to enlarge the capability of the congregation to accommodate diversity.

Seventh, the efforts at change became counterproductive as the level of discontent among a small number of new members was elevated, while the values, orientation, and attitudes of the other members remained unchanged. The result was not creative tension with the church council but rather destructive conflict between the majority of the old-timers on the one side and the newcomers and their newly won allies on the other.

Finally, both Dr. Warren and the Reverend Jack Reynolds overlooked the doctrine of original sin in their planning and failed to recognize the almost irresistible temptation that often entices laymen to play one minister against the other in a multiple staff situation. This is a not uncommon pattern in general, but it is frequently encountered when the membership includes both aggressive proponents of change and vigorous supporters of custom, tradition, and the status quo.

In reflecting on this experience three years later, Jack Reynolds commented to Dr. Warren, "At the time, I saw you being used by the old-timers to preserve their power, and I felt I was being used by the same group who were looking for a scapegoat. I sincerely believed that you were being faithful and obedient in responding to your call as a Christian minister, and I also sincerely believed I was being faithful and obedient as I sought to encourage a group of new and progressive leaders who were concerned about the mission of First Church. It never occurred to me that they were going to ask for your resignation or that it would end up with all three of us resigning and the Old Guard still in control!"

"I'm glad we're still friends, Jack," said Bill Warren, "but the key question is not, Were we faithful and obedient? The key question in what we did at First Church is a very simple one. How stupid can a pair of ministers be and still serve the Lord?"

## II

"I simply can't understand why Dave failed so completely on this assignment. When he was asked to go into the Birchdale community, I thought they were picking one of the best organizers in the country." This comment came from a puzzled denominational executive who was discussing a problem with two other men over a cup of coffee. One of the men was an action-oriented pastor in a large midwest city and also chairman of the denomination's committe on metropolitan ministries in that city. The third man was a professional social worker who had specialized in community organization and now taught at one of the state universities.

They were talking about the failure of an effort to organize the all-white, working-class Birchdale neighborhood on the city's north side. About eighteen months earlier, a newly organized group of residents, led by two young clergymen, had approached the denomination for help. This group asked the denomination to provide a professional community organizer for the Birchdale Community Association for two years. After several meetings three denominations agreed to provide 80 percent of the necessary funds if the residents would guarantee the other 20 percent. After this agreement was reached, the Association leaders selected David Cole as their man. He came with impressive recommendations. Following seminary graduation he had spent five years as the pastor of a small, inner-city congregation in a racially changing, northern urban community. When he came, the congregation was all white. When he left, Negroes constituted over one half of the membership and occupied a fourth of the leadership positions. Dave had spent the next two years organizing voter-registration drives in Mississippi. This was followed by a period as an organizer in the black ghetto of Cleveland's east side where he twice had worked in the mayoralty elections on behalf of Carl B. Stokes.

"I guess I was as surprised and baffled as anyone else when the Birchdale Association fired Dave," admitted the pastor to his two colleagues. "I thought that with his experience and know-how he was the perfect choice. Perhaps your evaluation will shed some light on this for us," he said, turning to the university professor.

"While my evaluation is not quite finished, I think I can offer a few comments on this question," was the response. "In simple terms, what you're asking is why did the Birchdale Community Association fire Dave Cole when he still had eight months to go on a two-year contract.

"In simple terms the answer is very clear. He cut his own throat.

"To be more precise," continued the university professor, "he made so many mistakes that anyone who wanted to get rid of him or to reduce the influence of the Birchdale Association had plenty of ammunition.

"In my opinion his biggest problem was his inability to define his role and adjust his tactics accordingly. As far as I can discover, Dave always conveyed the impression that he thought of himself as an enabler, as a change agent who enabled the people in the community to develop their own leadership potential and to determine their own destiny.

"His tactics, however, were inconsistent with that role. He used the tactics of the prophet who is primarily concerned with focusing the spotlight of public opinion on evil practices. I believe Dave is temperamentally cut out to be a dramatic prophet in the Old Testament tradition rather than an organizer who can help the people develop their own potential. He might have been able to work for several years in Birchdale if he had chosen either role *and utilized the tactics appropriate to that role.*

"In addition to this role-tactics conflict, Dave made a

25

half-dozen other mistakes, any two of which were sufficient to get him fired. First, he kept trying to define the issues in social and racial terms instead of in economic terms. Second, he apparently was completely unaware of the inter-relationships between several of the ethnic and nationality associations and the mayor's office. When he identified the mayor as an enemy, he alienated many of the ethnic leaders who have lived in Birchdale for years. Third, he identified the wrong enemy. He kept talking about the labor unions, city hall, and the landlords as the enemy. In Birchdale over two thirds of the residents in the labor force are union members, and there are at least three hundred city employees in that community. In addition, in at least five hundred of those two- and three-flat buildings the owner lives in one of the apartments in the building. Those people see themselves as landlords and know the problems that go with being a landlord in that kind of neighborhood.

"Dave saw the problems of this community from a sharply different perspective than that of the residents. Instead of asking them where they hurt, he told them where they hurt. For example, Dave was right, the schools in Birchdale are not doing a good job of preparing the kids to live in a racially integrated society or to deal with the forces of change. This is an important concern. The number-one worry of the parents, however, was the sale of drugs in the high school and junior high school. While Dave also was greatly concerned with this problem, in an effort to maintain a relationship with the kids he concealed his concern about the drug scene. When he talked with the kids, he talked from an agenda of racial and social concerns and education while the kids talked about the hypocrisy of their parents who have liquor in the house all of the time, but are down on drugs. When he talked with the parents, Dave talked about the failure of the schools in educational terms and the parents were talking about the failure of the schools to control the drug problem.

"This is not to say Dave was wrong about the issues he identified; it is simply that he was always talking about what the residents saw as second-priority concerns.

"A fourth mistake he made was in not doing his homework. He believed everything he read in the newspapers or heard on the grapevine. A lot of this turned out not to be true and it hurt Dave's credibility in the community. Twice he was publicly caught being wrong in his facts, once on the transfer of a teacher and once on that deal about a business agent misusing union members' dues. In either case a couple of hours of homework could have saved him a red face.

"Fifth, Dave never really tried to develop and utilize the skills of the residents and build alliances. It is worth noting that in every case when the Birchdale Association needed legal counsel, they went outside the community for a lawyer. On at least five occasions opponents of the Birchdale Association used a lawyer from that community in their dispute with Dave and the Association.

"Finally, and perhaps most important of all, Dave has a tendency not to follow through on what he starts. He switches from one new toy to another. A lot of people are convinced that if Dave had done as good a job on getting out the vote on election day as he did in getting people registered to vote that the Association's candidate for the city council last May would have been elected instead of losing by thirty-one votes. This same failure to follow through showed up in the Vine Street playground. Dave was the key man in blocking the proposed sale of that property by the Park District, but nothing was ever done to develop it as a playground. Today it is a field filled with waist-high weeds." [1]

### III

"Public housing in this town is never going to get out from under the thumb of the real estate interests and serve poor people unless we get a director for the Housing Authority who has the guts to stand up to the vested interests in this city, who has the administrative and the technical ability to run a good operation, and who has the interests of the poor at heart!" With this emotional statement Jim White got to the point of his luncheon appointment with Dick Brown.

Jim and two other community leaders had called Dick and asked to have lunch together. The three of them had been delegated by a coalition of civic committees to persuade Dick Brown to apply for the soon-to-be-vacated post of director of the Metropolitan Housing Authority. Dick was the executive secretary of the local Citizens' Planning and Housing Committee, a nonprofit group concerned with metropolitan planning, open housing, and related issues in a large metropolitan center in the midwest. Dick held a master's degree in public administration and had over twenty years of professional experience in public affairs. He was a committed Christian, an active Baptist layman, a tenacious champion of the underdog, and a very capable administrator who saw his vocation as enabling people to help themselves.

After securing pledges of support from Jim White and dozens of other civic leaders, Dick agreed to have his name placed before the Board of the Metropolitan Housing Authority as a candidate for the position of director. He was appointed, and the newspapers hailed his selection as a major forward step in putting new life into the city's public housing program.

Twenty-seven months later he was fired.

What happened?

By the time he was installed as director of the Housing Authority, Dick Brown had developed a four-point action program. The first step was to comply with the Civil Rights Act of 1968 which stated that as a matter of national policy public housing funds shall not be used to build housing on sites that would perpetuate racial ghettos. This meant a shift to scattered-site housing and aroused the hostility of whites who were afraid of blacks and of middle-class blacks who fear the influx into their neighborhoods of poor people of any color.

Dick's second goal was to encourage the active participation of the residents of public housing in policy formulation for the Authority. After all, they were the ones who were most affected by the policies of the Housing Authority. This offended several of the commissioners of the Housing Authority, a half-dozen former members of the Authority, and some of the people who had urged his appointment.

His third objective was to upgrade the quality of the personnel employed by the Housing Authority.

The fourth point on his program was to work out a schedule with the Federal Department of Housing and Urban Development, the local and state highway engineers, and the city's urban renewal department that would coordinate the construction of additional low-rent housing with the displacement of low-income families by highway and renewal projects. Dick hoped to be able to develop a coordinated approach to guarantee that housing would be available immediately to low- and low-middle-income families when they were to be displaced by a clearance program.

Twenty-one months after his appointment, a motion to fire Dick failed by a 4 to 3 vote. Six months later, with the appointment of one new commissioner the vote was 4 to 2 in support of a motion to fire Dick. One of his former supporters abstained from voting, although his vote would not have changed the result.

This action was greeted by a continuous seventy-two-hour protest by the recently organized Tenants' Union, by a three-day wildcat strike by one third of the Authority's employees, and by a rash of letters to the editor of both metropolitan newspapers.

What went wrong?

One explanation is that serving as director of a public agency in a large central city today is a guaranteed "no win" undertaking.

Another is that Dick Brown violated several of the basic principles of the process of planned change, and this caused his dismissal.

Perhaps his four gravest mistakes were these. First, he failed to distinguish between moral support and legitimacy. As director of the Housing Authority, Dick could not function very long without a supporting group which could give to him and his goals the aura of legitimacy. Only the commissioners could do this. The tenants, the employees, and the liberal groups in the metropolitan area could give him moral support, but they could not legitimatize his goals and his tactics. Only the commissioners could do that, and Dick made practically no effort to secure their continuing support after his appointment.

A second consideration that contributed to Dick's downfall was his definition of the word "compromise." To him, this was a dirty word, a sign of weakness and failure, rather than a normal and acceptable part of the political process.

Within two years his unwillingness to accept proposals for altering his goals and his absolute unwillingness to take anyone else's advice on the best tactics to achieve these goals had alienated the two traditional supporters of public housing—the labor unions and the professional social workers. Likewise, his unalterable support for the Tenants' Union divided another large part of his natural support, the tenants and the commissioners.

His third mistake was his failure to encourage his supporters to organize and to work to improve the climate for public housing in the metropolitan area. By the time Dick was appointed, public housing had had a stigma attached to it for years. Many of his plans were doomed to failure unless the climate of public opinion could be changed and the supporting group favoring more public housing was greatly enlarged.

Finally, his failure to deal with any of the political realities of life meant that in nearly three years he was able to secure the necessary municipal approval for only one scattered-site project of twelve units. For the same reasons he was never able to launch his program for the coordination of the construction of new housing with the displacement of residents from clearance projects. While he denied it vehemently, the heads of the other public agencies saw this as a move to use their functions as a lever for the placement of black families in white suburbs.

When it was all over, one of his old friends commented, "You may not give him an A for political acumen and tact, but you can't fault Dick Brown for his motives. His intentions were always the very best."

That is an accurate statement. It is also true, however, that a well-known and heavily traveled road is paved with good intentions. Little could be achieved by Dick's adding to the length of that road or improving the quality of the pavement.

These three incidents illustrate some of the pitfalls in the path of the advocate of intentional change. They suggest that he must be concerned with his goals and with the moral implications of both his strategy and his tactics. In addition to having laudable goals and noble motives, it can be helpful if he understands the nature of change, the process of planned social change, the use of power in the change process, the place of conflict, and the critical importance of change in organizations and institutions as well as in people. Perhaps a good beginning point is to look first at the nature of change.

# 2

# The Nature of Change

In May of 1949 only 12 percent of the people in Baltimore watched television. A year later more residents of Baltimore watched television than listened to the radio. Jack Benny's national Hooper rating was 27 in 1947. Three years later it had dropped slightly to 25.3. By 1954, however, it had plunged to 5.8.

In 1961 President John F. Kennedy declared the United States would place a man on the moon before the end of the decade. In July, 1969, the feat was accomplished.

In 1964 President Lyndon B. Johnson declared "unconditional war" on poverty. During the next several years the number of persons in the United States living below "the poverty line" dropped from 36 million in 1964 to 24.3 million in 1969, and the proportion of the total population living in poverty dropped from 17.3 to 12.2 percent during this period. In 1970, however, the number of persons living in poverty increased 1.2 million or 5.1 percent.[1]

These three illustrations raise one of the issues that is of fundamental importance to the agent of change. This is the nature of change. It may be helpful to look at this subject from several different perspectives.

## Types of Change

In discussing the difficulties present in an analysis of violent change Henry Bienen used the comparison of a snowball and an avalanche.[2] Both represent change, but there is a vast difference in the nature of the change.

What is meant by the word "change"?

One approach is to suggest the various types of change that can be identified. One that is getting tremendous attention in every part of the world is *modernization*. This category includes many of the changes occurring in several of the new nations of Africa, the replacement of high-unit-cost mills by a steel company, the installation of plumbing in an old farmhouse in West Virginia, and the new facade that has been constructed on an old office building.

A second type can be called *transformation*. This category may include the change in the first-grade child between September and May as he learns to read and a whole new world is opened up for him, the replacement of the 120-acre Iowa cornfield by a 400-unit housing development, and the new convert to Christianity.

A third type of change can be distinguished as *survival adaptation*. This category includes the person who has been

34

ordered by his physician to reduce his weight by seventy pounds, the family-owned grocery store that has been converted to a supermarket style of operation, the seventy-year-old church composed of a congregation that lives two to ten miles from the meeting place and undertakes a new neighborhood-oriented ministry, and the private trade school that makes a radical change in its curriculum.

Another approach to the types of changes is what at first appears to be those that are internally motivated and those that are externally motivated.

Some people use an even simpler typology. In one category are those changes I favor. In the second are those I oppose.

The use of these categories to define types of change not only helps to explain what is meant when the word "change" is used, but also is a useful first step in examining the nature of change, revealing motivations, and understanding the reasons behind the varying reactions to change.

From a different perspective, Thomas R. Bennett has suggested four types of change. The first is a change in *structure*.[3] Nearly every organization reaches that day when it decides a change in structure is necessary. The reorganization in the Federal Government that produced the Department of Health, Education, and Welfare stands as one example. During the early 1970s more than a dozen Protestant denominations became involved in structure studies directed at reorganizing the relationships of agencies and people within the denomination. Reorganization studies have become a major indoor sport all across the nation today.

Frequently the pressures for a change in structure are

the result of stresses and strains produced by the combination of internal dissatisfactions and external trends, pressures, or criticisms. The series of proposals for the change in the structure of the National Council of Churches is a good illustration of this. In addition to dissatisfactions from within the Council and the member denominations, there have been external pressures, several of them in opposing directions, such as the national trend toward decentralization, the rising visibility and militancy of blacks and other minority groups, the criticism of the Council's public pronouncements and programs, the general leveling off of giving by churches to national denominational bodies, and the possibility of including the Roman Catholic Church in the United States as an active participant in the Council's operation.

The second type of change suggested by Bennett is a change in *technology*. This type of change tends to be easier to accomplish and to secure acceptance of than any of the other three types of changes. The American people accommodated very quickly and relatively easily to the changes occasioned by the introduction of television, as the Baltimore experience illustrates so clearly. In general, a change in technology will arouse the vigorous opposition of only a small number of people, while social changes often arouse the opposition of large numbers.

In looking at technological changes, however, it is useful to recognize a very basic distinction. The impact of technological change is much greater, and often far more traumatic, for persons who find their traditions, customs, skills, and perhaps even their sense of self-esteem challenged by the change. The introduction of electronic data-processing equipment to replace the old bookkeeping machines in a local government office probably will not create more than a ripple of interest in the property owner who finds his annual tax bill includes a punched card. At the other end of this process this technological change can and has caused some people to lose their jobs or to divorce their spouses or to walk out one evening, never to be seen again in that community.

The impact of technological change can be seen by reviewing the revolution in agriculture, the declining importance of the battleship or the manned bomber in warfare, or the addition of sound to Hollywood motion pictures. For some it is of minor importance, for others a welcome improvement and for many a devastating emotional experience.

A third type of change is a change in *behavior*. Changes in both structure and technology tend to produce changes in behavior, sometimes deliberately, often unintentionally, and frequently without any preconceived plan for dealing with these unexpected changes.

In looking at this type of change it is helpful to distinguish among the desired change in behavior or performance, the method or technique devised to achieve that hoped-for change, the various consequences that may be produced by this stimulus, and, most important of all, the probable effect on the people involved. Frequently the last two are neglected.

One of the most effective methods of influencing behavior in either an individual or an organization is by the questions that are asked in the reporting system. In World War

II the question most commonly asked to measure "progress" centered on the number of kilometers or miles the allied groups had advanced. In Vietnam "progress" was measured by a "body count." There are many who will argue that these two questions influenced the behavior patterns and performance of the troops.

The fourth type of change identified by Bennett concerns *assumptions and values.* Bennett emphasizes the importance of a group leader being able to identify *his own* values and assumptions. Unless he has clear insight into the values and assumptions that guide his own behavior, he may be not only an ineffective leader; he may be very destructive to others.

A change in values and assumptions is essential before the behavior of either an individual or an organization can be changed substantially. This is widely accepted in discussions about a change of behavior in individuals, but is often neglected in proposals for a change in the behavior or performance of an organization such as a labor union, a church, a school, a club, or a business.

A change in values and assumptions almost invariably is far more complex than it may first appear. Kurt Lewin emphasized that this is equivalent to a change in culture. He illustrated this point by the example of a carpenter who desires to become a watchmaker. Lewin pointed out that this requires more than for the carpenter to learn the skills of a watchmaker. Before he can function effectively and contentedly as a watchmaker, he has to acquire a whole new frame of reference or system for looking at his work. This means a change in habits, standards and values, *and the stabilization of this new frame of reference.*[4] (See Chapter 7 for an elaboration of this point.)

## Sources of Change

Another way of looking at the nature of change is to consider the sources of change.

This book is concerned primarily and almost entirely with planned change that is intentionally initiated or is a systematic response to external pressures. This involves a conscious decision and often, but not always, includes some consideration of the probable consequences of the actions involved in initiating change.

There are two types of change, in terms of the source, that are compatible with this approach. The first is the *internally motivated* decision. An example of this is the deliberate decision of an individual to resign from his job and seek other employment. The decision by the sixty-three-year-old farmer to sell his farm to a stranger and retire is another. The decision by old First Church to sell its downtown property and relocate in the suburbs is a third illustration. The decision by a community organization to build and manage a housing project in the neighborhood is another. The decision by a denominational board to develop a completely new approach to what traditionally has been labeled "Christian education" is a fifth illustration of intentional planned change.

In each of these examples the *primary* motivation for change comes from *within* the individual or organization. In each one, however, there are obviously external forces or pressures at work which have influenced the decision and over which the individual or the organization has little or no control. It is clear that what often appears to be internally motivated change usually is influenced by external consideration.

It is in this type of situation that the agent of change has the greatest opportunities to work for planned change.

A second source, which differs in degree rather than in absolute terms, is *externally motivated* change. An example of this is when the closing of a large defense installation near a small town in the South forced several motels to close. Another is when The Methodist Church and the Evangelical United Brethren Church merged to form a new denomination. This action soon forced several congregations which had carried the name "First EUB Church" for decades not only to change their name, but to redefine their purpose and role. When Amtrak was created to provide rail passenger service in the United States, this externally motivated change forced thousands of railroad employees to change employment. A fourth illustration of this type of change can be seen in the construction of the interstate highway system which caused many gasoline-station operators to change their business locations.

This type of change is basically the opposite of the internally motivated change. In this type the *primary* motivation for change is external, but internal considerations have a significant impact in the nature of the changes that occur in response to these external pressures.

In this type of change situation there remains the opportunity for *planned* change, but it is primarily a response to external forces, and the person concerned with intentional planned change has less control over the timing, the pace, and the range of alternatives than in the first type, where the motivation is primarily internal.

A third type of change in this range of categories is of a substantially different nature. This is change by indecision. In these situations it matters little whether the primary pressures for change are internal or external. The focus here is on the response to these forces for changes. A wide range of situations fall into this category. They include the person with a decaying tooth who postpones going to the dentist until all the alternatives except extraction have been eliminated. They include the leaders of the congregation in a changing situation who postpone action until the only alternative left is dissolution. They include the board of directors who ignore the implications of the dwindling sales of their product until it is too late to adapt or innovate. They include the community leaders who do nothing about the mounting discontent among the black residents until the week after the riot.

These are the situations which produce the greatest frustration for the advocate of planned change.

While this should not be interpreted as a discouraging comment, in contemporary American society most changes fall into the second or third of these three categories. This is a condition that can be less of a handicap to the agent of change if he recognizes its existence.

It appears, however, that the proportion of change that is either deliberately motivated from internal sources or is the response to deliberate change elsewhere is increasing.[5] In other words, the proportion of change that is a product of indecision or of "waiting to see what the future brings" is decreasing.

## Inside or Outside?

During the past few years there has been widespread discussion, especially among young people, "radicals," "old liberals," and the "New Left" about the viability of change by reform versus change by revolution. The reformers contend that it is possible to achieve the desired changes by working within the system. The revolutionaries have denied this. They contend that only by scrapping the existing institutions and structures of society will it be possible to achieve the necessary changes. Some contend, for example, that racism is so deeply engrained in America that it cannot be eradicated by reform, the present structures and the institutions must be replaced if racism is to be eliminated.

There is also the widely shared belief that significant changes cannot be expected to originate from within the organization. Some hold to this view because they are convinced the persons who have the power to accomplish the necessary changes will not voluntarily risk their power by advocating major changes in the system. Others agree with the conclusion, but for a different reason. They are convinced that tradition, precedent, and the institutionalized bureaucracy are so powerful that even the persons who are believed to hold great power actually are limited in the changes they can accomplish.[6]

This last point was illustrated by an incident in the political career of Senator Charles H. Percy of Illinois.

In an effort to discover why young people feel alienated from society, Senator Percy went on a five-day tour of nine Illinois campuses. He encountered great skepticism.

"I would really feel impotent if I were you," one student told him as they discussed whether even a senator can do much against the system. "And maybe you do," he concluded.

The "inside or outside" issue raises several questions for the individual who identifies himself as an advocate of intentional change. Does he plan to work for change from the inside? Or from the outside? The answer to this question will have a tremendous influence on the tactics he chooses.

If he chooses the revolutionary route, does he favor violent or nonviolent revolution?

Does he believe there is some central unitary "power structure" that is manipulating society? Or does he believe there really is no one who has complete absolute control and that to a substantial degree the organization or system runs itself?

Does he believe hatred is stronger than love as a force for change? Does he believe that the use of violence promotes progress or encourages repression?

These are only a few of the questions facing the agent of change as he chooses between "inside" and "outside."

This choice has been made more difficult in recent years because of the escalation of the rhetoric. One political observer noted this when he wrote, "Today's left has less a program for revolutionary change than a fondness for using revolutionary rhetoric and tactics to extract immediate concessions from the Establishment." [7]

In the United States today "revolution" has become increasingly a spectator sport rather than a viable alternative for change. One of the reasons for this is that violent revolution probably is impossible in a nation in which the military forces are under civilian control, in which both radio and television could be instantly co-opted by the government to oppose efforts to mobilize a revolutionary force, and in which an increasingly large number of people are seeing that the first victims of any attempt at violent revolution would be the proponents of violence.

Somewhat more subtle and perhaps more important reasons for doubting the viability of violent revolution in the United States today are two other factors. The first is that most of the political and social alienation that exists in the United States today is not of a radical revolutionary nature. The failure of the many attempts to develop an alliance between students and blue-collar workers is one example of this.

The other reason is that by its nature the United States Constitution was drawn to permit radical change without the disruptions of violent revolution. The contemporary black revolution has been consistent with the United States Constitution; it has been nurtured and assisted by the Constitution. Black revolutionaries have an ally, not an enemy, in the United States Constitution. The same is true of those seeking to enlarge the freedom of welfare mothers, students, the poor, the landless, the young, and the members of the military establishment.

The United States Constitution was the product of a rebellion against England, not of a revolution against the existing structures and systems of American society. As a result it has facilitated change and the enlargement of human freedom.

William Graham Sumner saw American history as a continuing series of conflicts between the democratic spirit of the country and the inherited institutions of the nation. Using this interpretation as a guide, it is easy to see the Civil War as a revolution, and possibly also the New Deal, but other changes have been the product of efforts to reform the institutions and structures of American society rather than revolutionary activities.

If one accepts this line of reasoning, it means that any revolutionary changes of the future probably will come from the right as an effort to restrict the continued diffusion of power in response to the democratic spirit of the nation. While these efforts may be clothed in the rhetoric of the left, they actually will be rightist in philosophy and intent. Like most other revolutions, this one would be supported more by the wealthy than by the poor.

This interpretation of American history also suggests that anyone advocating changes which are in harmony with the traditional democratic spirit of the nation will continue to work within the system which has a constitutional base for achieving these goals. Those who favor a restriction on human freedom, on participation, and on individual choice may have to turn to violent political revolution to accomplish and maintain the changes they desire.

The implications of this for the advocate of planned change are varied and too numerous to list here, but four should be lifted up for emphasis.

First, it means the question of "inside or outside" the

45

system will be determined by strategic rather than tactical considerations.

Second, for the reformer who chooses to work within the system it means that one of his primary tasks is to know the institution to be changed better than the ones who now control it know it. Here again it is obvious that the person who does his homework most thoroughly has a tremendous advantage over everyone else.

Third, if the agent of change is a reformer, as he examines his goals and tactics he should measure both goals and tactics against the criterion, "Will these make the system work better and are they in harmony with a democratic spirit?"

Finally, and perhaps most important, he should ask, "What are the alternatives for accomplishing this change?" This question removes the restrictions of the "either inside or outside" approach and places a third alternative on the agenda for consideration of the nature of change.

## The Third Alternative

"One of the governor's speech writers is on the telephone. He wants to know if you have any specific suggestions on how the state can help us and the other large cities. Next week the governor is addressing a national gathering of businessmen on the urban crisis, and he wants to offer some new ideas on how the states can begin to replace the role of the Federal Government in dealing with the crises in race relations, slums, education, traffic, poverty, air travel, crime, and similar issues. Do you have anything to suggest?"

As the mayor of a large midwest city looked up from his desk at the young assistant who had interrupted him, he responded to the question quickly, briefly, and without even the hint of a smile—"Tell him to send money."

There is a common belief among many of those who are interested in planned social change that the core of the answer is money. If the Congress would appropriate more money, the housing crisis could be relieved. If the churches would reallocate their financial resources from new church development or from the construction of religious buildings, this would help solve the problems of the poor. If another five billion dollars could be made available for law enforcement, the rising tide of crime and violence could be reversed. If the schools in the inner city had more money they could concentrate on education rather than serving as giant child-care centers.

There is an element of truth in each of those statements, but money alone is seldom the critical ingredient in the process of social change.

For the person who is affirmatively interested in improving the conditions of life, money is not the resource he needs. For the individual who is determined to humanize the world to make it a better place to live, money is not the tool he is seeking. For the Christian with a social conscience who recognizes the need to reform or change the structures and institutions of society which perpetuate inequality, injustice, poverty, racism, and violence, money is not the prime weapon in his arsenal. For the change agent "more of the same" is not the best alternative—and more money tends to buy more of the same. History is full of

47

examples of how the well-intentioned gift of money that was given to produce freedom resulted in greater tyranny and the expenditure made to reduce injustice produced new forms of injustice.

The historical record is overwhelmingly on the side of the argument that ideas, innovation, and an openness to new approaches to problem-solving are far more influential forces than dollars in the change process. Innovation constitutes an attractive third alternative to the traditional either-or approach of reform or revolution. Ideas are an essential and powerful force both in innovation and in preserving the status quo.

The *idea* that a propertyless adult man had as much right as the owner of property to vote for elected public officials changed the American political system.

The *idea* that the white man was superior to the black man built a social and economic system. The *idea* that the black man was the equal of the white man in the sight of God destroyed that economic system. A century later the *idea* that the black man should be treated as an equal of the white began to destroy a social system.

The *idea* that women are inferior to men has been the basis for one set of political, economic, social, and familial relationships. The *idea* that women are equal to men is creating and will continue to create a changed set of relationships in American society.

The *idea* that a sixteen- or a nineteen-year-old person is more than simply an object or a subject is beginning to create a sharply changed set of relationships between young persons and the judicial system, between young persons and the institutions of formal education, between young persons and the traditional leaders of the local church, and between young persons and their parents. Ideas such as these have changed and will continue to change American society. Ideas such as these are the most important single force for social change. Ideas such as these can be generated and can flow only in a society that has an open-ended view of itself and of the future.

In the last third of the nineteenth century, the most dramatic and impressive ideas that changed American society were expressed as technological *inventions*. Perhaps the best illustration of this can be seen in the urbanization of the nation.

Historians sometimes label the last third of the nineteenth century as the period in American history marked by the rise of the city. This is a valid designation. In 1860 there were only 16 cities in this nation with 50,000 or more residents. By 1900 there were 80, five times as many. The number with a population in excess of 25,000 rose from 35 in 1860 to 160 in 1900.

This was the era when millions of young people, who were born and reared in rural America, responded to the glamor of the city and chose the excitement of the city over the drudgery of the country.

This also was the period of a huge wave of immigration from Europe. From 1881 to 1900, nine million immigrants came to these shores from Europe. While a large number of them settled on the farms of the midwest, the great plains, and Texas, millions chose to build a new life in the cities of this rapidly growing nation.

This was not only the era of the rise of the city, it also was the era of great inventions, and the two are very closely interrelated. In the brief span of about a dozen years, seven major inventions appeared which made it possible for the modern American city to develop. These seven inventions were the telephone (1876), the skyscraper (1880), the incandescent lamp (1880), the electric trolley car (1885), the subway (1886), the automobile (1889), and the electric elevator (1889).

Without these seven inventions today's urban centers would be vastly different than the cities we know. The skyscraper and the elevator made possible the high-density central business district. The electric trolley, the subway, and the automobile made it possible to bring together in a relatively small land area the huge daytime population, and then for these workers to disperse over a wide area to their homes. The telephone provided the system necessary for communication among a large concentration of people. The incandescent lamp provided the light necessary for the conducting of business, the movement of goods and people, and the safety of the urban community.

These seven inventions were extremely influential in shaping the cities that rose in the last third of the nineteenth century, and they also shaped the cities that we know today in the last third of the twentieth century. Without these and other inventions urban life would be far different today.

The next phase in the urbanization of the nation was one of refinement and growth. In general terms this period can be defined as extending from 1890 to 1960. During these seven decades the country's urban population rose from 22 million to 113 million, while the rural population increased by only one half, from 41 million to 66 million. The number of urban places with a population of 5,000 or more rose from 229 in 1860 to 905 in 1900, to 3,393 in 1960 to nearly 5,000 in 1970.

Basically this was a period of urban expansion along the same pattern that had developed in the last third of the nineteenth century. It was a period when the ideas, concepts, and inventions that had emerged before 1890 were refined and improved.

There were relatively few new inventions that had a major impact on the city. The electric starter for the automobile greatly expanded the number of people who could ignore public transportation and depend on a private vehicle. The airplane altered the habits and needs of the businessman. The electric refrigerator, the development of low-cost frozen foods, and the supermarket changed the shopping habits of the housewife. The invention of synthetic fabrics, mechanical air conditioning, and new medicines affected the life-style of the individual more than they influenced social patterns. Television had a profound impact on the entertainment industry and the political scene. This has altered the role of the central business district and altered the operation of the political process.

While these and other inventions have had an impact on the city, the basic pattern from 1890 to 1960 was one of refining and expanding old ideas. This seven-decade era was one in which it was reasonably safe to expect that tomorrow would be like yesterday—only bigger and better.

With the exception of the airplane, there were no important new inventions that directly greatly altered the face of the American city. The changes that occurred were the changes produced by growth and by the refinement,

51

improvement, and wider use of the basic inventions that emerged during the nineteenth century. Portland cement, for example, has been the basic construction ingredient in building urban America. It was invented in 1824. Most of the basic inventions that provided the foundation for the industrialization, and thus the urbanization, of America were produced in the 1800s.

The one outstanding exception to this generalization is the series of inventions that altered American agriculture. The technological revolution that occurred on the farms of the nation between 1935 and 1970 reduced the *proportion* of the American population living on farms from 26 percent to 5 percent. In actual numbers, the farm population dropped from 32.2 million in 1935 to 10 million in 1970.

The changes produced by these technological advances can be seen all across rural America, but they have been felt even more acutely in the cities. While 1,500 rural counties have registered a sharp decrease in population because of the technological changes in American agriculture, 300 urban counties now include an additional 50 million residents who otherwise would still be living on farms.

## From Invention to Innovation

The technological advances that occurred in agriculture between 1935 and 1970 offer several instructive lessons to the change-oriented individual.

First, the critical element in this process was not the series of inventions. It was the spirit of innovation that moved farmers to exploit old inventions—such as the gasoline engine—and produced a demand and a market for new ones—such as chemical weed-killers.

Second, this spirit of innovation was fostered by one of the largest groups of professional change agents in the world's history. They were the county agricultural agents and the teachers of vocational agriculture in the high schools. The Smith-Lever Act of 1914 provided for the cooperative agricultural extension program. During the 1930s and 1940s this program helped finance a staff of 12,000 professional innovators in agriculture. The Smith-Hughes Act of 1917 authorized the use of federal funds for vocational education *including farming*. In the 1930s and 1940s there were 18,000 to 20,000 "ag teachers" accelerating the pace of innovation in agriculture.

A third important lesson from this experience for the contemporary change agent was the style of these professional innovators. The effective ones placed the primary emphasis on responding to the farmer's needs as identified and articulated by the farmer. Instead of trying to persuade the farmer to experiment with a new seed or to plow his fields following contour lines or to shift to the artificial insemination of his cattle, they responded to expressed needs. The effective persons in these professions carried the image, not of salesmen, but of helpers. They did not try to "sell" radically new ideas to reluctant farmers. They responded with constructive suggestions to felt needs.

They held an open-ended view of the future which they did not attempt to force on others, but which enabled them to see and to suggest new ways of solving old problems.

Finally, the experiences of these county agents and "ag teachers" illustrate the nature of innovation, the sources

**53**

of innovation and several of the requirements for introducing new ideas into a status quo–oriented system or organization.

## The Nature of Innovation

"Almost nothing new works" is a common expression among innovative persons. This phrase is not spoken, however, in a defeatist tone of voice, but rather in simple recognition of the fact that innovation is a high-risk venture.

Peter Drucker has identified three major risks in innovation.[8]

The first is that it will make obsolete current practices and patterns of operation.

The second is that it will fail.

The third is that it will succeed—but in succeeding it may produce unforeseen consequences that create new problems. A simple contemporary illustration of this is the local church that deliberately adopts an innovative approach to ministering to young persons. When these efforts do succeed they frequently produce a deep sense of hostility and alienation among members in the thirty-to-fifty-five age range. Another example is the rise of the private pension funds in industry and business. This is one of the great social innovations of the post–World War II era. Unless the employee has vested rights in the pension fund, however, this has had the unplanned consequence of greatly inhibiting his occupational mobility or of misleading him into a false sense of security.

These risks help explain why innovation normally is resisted by any organization or institution. The more rigid the organizational or bureaucratic structure, the greater the resistance to innovation. This is why military organizations have tended to plan for using the weapons of the last war in preparing for the next war.

A second characteristic of innovation is that, unlike reform and revolution, the focus is on the new, not on the old. The revolutionary will argue that the existing welfare system must be abolished, and his energies will be devoted to toppling the society that has permitted the growth of such an unjust system. The reformer will contend that it can be overhauled and made to work more effectively. The innovator will devote his efforts to developing a new method of responding to the needs of the poor, the oppressed, and the victims of social disaster. His emphasis is on adding to the resources of society, rather than on destroying or reforming old programs and methods.

The innovator is not an opponent of the old; he is a proponent of the new. There is a vast difference between these two positions. One of the critical distinctions is that the proponent of the new seldom is trapped, as so often happens to the opponent of the old, into becoming part of a veto bloc opposed to any change.

A third important characteristic of innovation is that it tends to avoid some of the ideological problems that often produce a polarizing paralysis that halts all efforts at change from within. As Drucker emphasizes, the innovator usually is free to utilize traditional values, beliefs, and institutions.

Finally, and it is difficult to overemphasize this, innovation, unlike reform and revolution, has a built-in dynamic characteristic that tends to create and perpetuate an openness to change. The historical record demonstrates rather conclusively that unsuccessful revolutions reinforce the status quo while successful revolutions tend simply to institutionalize a new status quo. Likewise, with passage of time, reform efforts tend to become an end rather than a means. New reform movements must be initiated to correct the deficiencies of the earlier reform efforts. The recent history of two great reforms of the 1930s—aid to dependent children and public housing—are examples of this.

By contrast, the sources of innovation and the requirements for successful innovation tend to create a climate favorable to an ethic of change.[9]

## Opening the Door to Innovation

The person who is interested in change through innovation has many choices to make. One is the choice between either acting as an innovator and seeking to press for change through the introduction and implementation of new ideas or acting as a facilitator of change and seeking to increase the degree of openness to innovation in the entire organization. While the two are not mutually incompatible roles, they are distinctly different, and since both are time consuming, it is unlikely one person will function effectively in both roles at the same point in history.

A high school teacher, for example, may be interested in changing the purpose of the classroom examination from the contemporary notion that it is a means of ranking or grading students back into the earlier concept of the examination as a part of the learning process.

In planning a strategy for this change it makes a great difference to this teacher whether the object of his immediate concern about the place of written examinations is the student in his classes or the school system in which he operates.

If it is the former, he will be primarily concerned with his students, their values, beliefs, and attitudes in regard to examinations, and the formative experiences they have had in previous years which have produced and reinforced their current views of the place of examinations. His secondary concern may be with the schools, classrooms, and teachers to which his students have been exposed in previous years.

On the other hand, if this teacher directs his concern to the place and image of examinations in the high school in which he teaches, his primary concern probably will be with the faculty and administration of the high school rather than with his students. His secondary concern probably will not be with the practices of the elementary schools which feed students into his high school, but rather with the universities and colleges which train the teachers and administrators in high schools and which set the values for high school. (The values of the teachers and administrators tend to be influenced by the next system above them in the educational hierarchy while the attitudes of the students tend to be shaped by the next system below them in the system.)

There are two relevant points in this illustration. The first and the most obvious is that the teacher who seeks to change the attitude of his students toward examinations is doomed to a frustration-filled career unless there are similar changes taking place elsewhere throughout the entire educational system.

The second is that if he is serious about changing the

system, he should recognize the importance of a favorable climate for creativity and innovation. In some organizations the climate is far more favorable to change than in others. The effective change agent not only recognizes this, he also is aware of the characteristics that are a part of the creative organization, and he knows how to nurture the growth of these characteristics.

Among the characteristics that usually can be found in the creative organization that is open to innovation are these twelve:[10]

1. The primary orientation of the organization and of the persons in the organization is to the contemporary social scene, rather than to yesterday or to the perpetuation of the organization.

2. There is a profound awareness that problems do exist.

3. Throughout the organization the primary focus is on people and people's needs, rather than on the product or service the organization has been producing or on the preservation or maintenance of the organization.

This emphasis on people and their needs enables the creative organization to include the clientele as part of the decision-making team. The feedback from the clientele is essential for the self-modifying element in creative decision-making.

4. Within the creative organization the emphasis is on problem-solving, and especially on solving social problems, rather than on institutional maintenance or on "keeping the operation running smoothly."

5. The persons in the creative organization are clearly aware of the importance, relevance, and availability of knowledge from a variety of disciplines that can be utilized

by the organization in fulfilling its purpose and achieving its goals. The creative organization displays an unusual capability or flair for utilizing and applying the knowledge, wisdom, and insights of other disciplines. Likewise, there is an awareness that the beliefs, values, and attitudes of people determine the limitations on the mobilization and utilization of knowledge.

6. Within the creative organization there is a continuing effort to monitor the pace of change that can be accommodated before the benefits of change are outweighed by the costs of disruption.

7. There is a built-in self-evaluation process in the creative organization which is designed to test the present operation against the definition of purpose. Without this, the normal institutional pressures subvert the operation, and the means to an end become ends or goals in themselves.

8. Within the creative organization there is a widespread recognition and acceptance of the fact that frequently the organization will be attempting to reach a goal which will be changing during the period of the effort to reach it.

9. The financial administration of the creative organization places the primary emphasis on expenditures, costs, output, and program rather than on receipts, revenues, and input.

10. The personnel administration of the creative organization reflects an attempt to maximize the problem-solving capability of the organization rather than simply an effort to manage the time, compensation, and control of a labor force.

11. When new ideas are proposed, the leaders within the

organization know the most potentially fruitful points of intervention into the ongoing life and operation of the organization.

12. In the creative organization every person is, to at least a limited extent, a generalist, and to an outsider the organization appears to resemble a series of interlocking small groups with individuals moving from one position to another, both within and between groups.

In an era of increasing specialization, the natural tendency is for each person to specialize, to occupy a narrowly defined niche within his subdivision of the larger organization. In the creative organization a deliberate effort is made to reverse this tendency and to enable each person to see the organization, its goals, and its problems from the perspective of other members of the organization. Creativity and innovation tend to be fostered as people are able to look at the operation of the organization from a variety of perspectives.

The reader of this list of twelve characteristics of the creative may have one or more of several reactions. He may see this as interesting but irrelevant to his situation. He may conclude that each item is too subjective to have any meaning for him. He may pass it off as a lot of garbage. Or he may use it as a checklist to determine whether his organization is structured to encourage or to discourage creativity and innovation.

The innovation-oriented change agent is more likely to look at such a list and ask how these characteristics can be built into his organization to increase its openness to innovation and to encourage a more favorable climate for creative innovation.

In simple terms, how does one structure an openness to change and to new ideas into an organization?

One part of the answer to that question is to develop a list of the characteristics that will encourage creativity in that organization.

A second part of the answer is to make those changes which will tend to nurture these characteristics. For example, the questions asked in the reporting system have a tremendous impact on the performance of both the individual and of the organization. Questions that measure only activities (how many meetings did you attend last month?) may prove to be a diversion from purpose. The questions asked in reporting should reflect the basic purpose and the goals of the organization. Thus, one way to achieve the goal of creativity is to ask questions about creativity in the reporting process.

Likewise, the questions asked in the reporting system influence the openness of an organization to change and to new ideas. For example, what would be the effect on local churches if the annual report to the denomination was limited to a score of questions, three of which were these: What new approach to ministry did this congregation undertake during the past year? What program component was dropped or eliminated as functionally obsolete or as no longer appropriate for this congregation? What component of the total program was changed because of the identification of new or different needs among the people?

Obviously the impact of these questions will be greater if they are asked a year in advance.

Thus, changes in the questions asked in the reporting

system could encourage the growth of the first four items in the above list. In-service training programs for members of the organization can be used to encourage the emergence of the fifth and sixth items on this list. A persistent effort to define and emphasize the definition of purpose in every effort at evaluation will tend to strengthen the seventh point on this list. The use of program budgeting will reinforce characteristics numbered seven through eleven. A not uncommon means of encouraging the growth of the broader perspective called for in item twelve is to ask each person to spend two to four hours at another's task each month.

Often one of the most important dimensions of a change agent's job may be to foster creativity by asking questions rather than by suggesting answers.

### "You Can't Legislate Morality!"

One of the favorite arguments of opponents of internally motivated, intentional change is, "But you can't legislate morality!"

As recently as 1952, Tennessee Senator Estes Kefauver, who was an active candidate for the Democratic nomination for the presidency, sought to explain his vote against federal anti-lynching and fair employment legislation on the grounds "because frankly I do not think it would achieve this end. It is difficult to legislate a change in the habits of people." [11]

During the past two decades it has been demonstrated repeatedly that this is a false statement. Without going into a definition of morality, it is clear that legislation can change the habits and behavior of people. It may be helpful to distinguish between attitudes and actions in this discussion. It clearly is possible to change people's actions by legislation, and apparently attitudes change as behavior changes.

Among the most highly visible examples of this are fair employment legislation, open housing legislation, and the legislation (usually preceded by law suits) which eliminated the racial or religious quotas in various educational institutions.

A lengthening list of public opinion polls and attitudinal studies indicates there has been a major change in both the openly expressed attitudes and the more reserved opinions of the American population on a series of issues where legislation has changed behavior. While it is impossible to prove a direct cause-and-effect relationship, those who believe cigarette smoking causes lung cancer probably will be persuaded that legislation can change attitudes as well as behavior and that a change in behavior tends to produce a parallel change in attitudes.

Legislation not only can change both actions and attitudes; it also is one means of accelerating—or of retarding—the pace of change.

## The Pace of Change

On April 22, 1918, the Montana State Council of Defense called for suppression of the German language in public and private schools throughout the state. By noon the following day the state university at Missoula had discontinued all its classes in German.[12]

Between 1915 and 1922 the proportion of all high school

pupils in the United States taking German dropped from over 24 percent to less than 1 percent.

These two related incidents illustrate how rapidly change can occur. A quarter of a century ago Kurt Lewin pointed out that periods of social change differ from periods of stability, and the faster the pace of change, the greater the differences between a period of change and a period of relative social stability.

In normal times and under normal conditions the pace of internally motivated intentional change tends to be slow. During a crisis, it is relatively easy to accelerate the pace of change. In normal times it would take at least a year or two for a state agency to change the curriculum in a state university. In April, 1918, this was accomplished in less than twenty-four hours.

The obvious point is that during the period of a perceived crisis, the pace of change can be speeded up tremendously. It matters more that a crisis is perceived than whether a crisis actually exists.

A second method for hastening the pace of planned change is to deliberately encourage an increase in the level of discontent with the status quo.

A third approach, which is the other side of the same picture, is to increase the attractiveness of the proposed goal.

A fourth method is to increase the number and frequency of discussions, both formal and informal, about the proposed course of action. Most changes require a quantity of talk or "milling around," and the time span for fulfilling this requirement often can be shortened, thus accelerating the pace of change.

Another related means of stepping up the pace of change is to focus attention, not on the proposed change, but on building up the level of trust. The higher the trust level, the easier it is for planned change to take place.

A sixth method of speeding up the pace of change is to minimize precedent, tradition, and custom and to start "fresh" with as few of the encumbrances of the past as possible. Zero budgeting, in which zeroes replace all the numbers in last year's budget, is one expression of this concept.

Finally, it is possible to increase the pace of change by giving high priority to the early enlargement of the supporting group of persons who favor the proposal and who have some form of personal interest in seeing the change adopted.

It should be apparent to every advocate of planned change that these methods of speeding up the pace can be reversed and used to slow down the pace of change just as legislation can be used to accelerate or to retard the pace of change.

## Expectations and Change

In recent years research in education has suggested that one of the many reasons why public schools fail the poor is the expectation of substandard performance which pervades the atmosphere of most slum schools. There is a tendency for both students and parents to internalize the expectations of teachers and administrators.[13]

The Peace Corps has operated on the principle that a person can do more than he believes he can. Acting on this principle the Peace Corps has consistently pushed the individual beyond the limits he has set for himself as a self-sufficient person, as an enabler, as an agent of change, and as a community developer. Success breeds self-confidence and pushes out the individual's limits.

Outward Bound follows the same principle by challenging individuals to live in the wilderness and to be self-sufficient. The individual is expected to be able to climb mountains—and usually he succeeds.

Despite the contemporary adverse comments about military service, there is considerable persuasive evidence that the military does provide significant opportunities for personal growth for many individuals. The training procedures in use in all branches of the armed services do assume maximum potential for personal growth by each individual. The best example of this is in basic training where it is assumed that every individual can master the content of the basic training course. It is a nongraded system built on the expectation that everyone will pass, although some individuals may need extra attention or additional time.

In Project 100,000 the military establishment undertook an experiment in basic adult education directed at persons who were below the minimum requirements of the services. By September, 1968, 140,000 men had entered the armed forces, all of whom would have been rejected if the traditional pattern of expectations had been followed.[14]

For several years a number of Protestant seminaries helped to convey the expectation to students that they would be dissatisfied with the parish ministry and either would be unhappy or would drop out of the professional ministry.

On the other hand several Lutheran seminaries conveyed the expectation that their students would enter the parish ministry and find this to be a fulfilling and rewarding experience. To a very substantial degree both sets of expectations were fulfilled.

The obvious point of these illustrations is that a change agent's effectiveness will be determined, in part at least, by his expectations.

This is another insight which was clarified by the pioneering work of Kurt Lewin. Using the term "aspiration" rather than "expectation," Lewin and others have demonstrated two very relevant points about the importance of expectations. First, success in reaching a goal tends to cause the individual to raise the goal. They proved there is merit in the old adage "Success breeds success."

Second, and more subtle and perhaps more important to the change agent, these researchers pointed out that to succeed in achieving the initial goal a person must aspire to attain it, *but he is unlikely to aspire unless he can see that success is possible,* that others in the same group are succeeding. It also follows that failure to achieve a goal results in a lowering of expectations and the setting of a lower goal.[15]

One of the most common examples of this second point could be found in several Northern cities during the 1950s when the largest employers of Negro college graduates were the municipal bus system and the post office.

As the advocate of change reflects on the importance of expectations, he can see the value both of helping to raise the level of expectation and, even more crucial, of helping people achieve the victories or successes that affirm their expectations and raise their level of aspiration.

The other side of the expectations subject is the response of people. One of the most significant elements of the nature of change is the response to change. This can be seen by looking at three different dimensions of the subject: the response of people to change, the response of institutions to change, and the response of both people and institutions to a crisis.

### Responses of People to Change

"What are you, personally, doing to end the war in Asia?" challenged a bearded youth as he listened to a United States senator speak during one of the latter's weekend trips to his home state.

"We hope to be able to halt the war in Vietnam by cutting off the appropriations that finance the United States' involvement in that conflict," answered the senator somewhat defensively.

"Why don't you do that now?" demanded another member of the audience.

"We can't until we have the votes," responded the senator. "Today we do not have the necessary number of votes in the Senate to support that action. Until we do it would be fruitless to introduce such legislation."

This exchange illustrates two of the many responses to a call for change. The first, represented by this United States senator, is the natural tendency of a social system to respond to any demand for change by following its normal procedures. This should not be construed as a criticism. It is simply a statement of a normal response. A social system's reaction to a call for change normally will be as a function of its regular procedures. Unless there is a malfunction in the system, such as a *coup d'etat* or a perceived crisis, that will be the nature of the response. Anyone who expects otherwise either is naïve or believes in frequent miracles.

A second type of response to pressure for change is illustrated by the question from the second member of the audience. "Why don't you do that now?" he asked. His impatience represents another of the common responses to change.

These two responses do not begin to exhaust the tremendous variety of reactions human beings have to change or the prospect of change. A few of the other responses are represented by such words, as fear, anger, disgust, confusion, violence, amazement, shock, resistance, disbelief, apathy, misunderstanding, joy, questions, incredulity, withdrawal, openness, boycott, and a variety of efforts to personify the cause of the proposed change.

Most of these responses can be placed in one of four categories—neutral, negative, affirmative, or counterproductive.

It may be helpful for an advocate of change to examine these varied responses as he seeks to improve his effectiveness as an agent of change.

Most of the discussions concerning people's reactions to change have tended to focus on resistance to change and to ignore the other types of responses. This is a natural pattern, since change-oriented persons can be expected to be primarily concerned with the opposition. It may be more helpful to look at the whole range of responses instead of concentrating on a single category.

While space prohibits an extensive discussion of this issue, six points stand out that do merit the thoughtful attention of the advocate of planned change.

The first, and perhaps the most obvious, is that it helps to be able to anticipate the probable response to a proposal for change and to be prepared to deal with that response.

Closely related to this is the fact that in most situations the initial reaction of most people to a proposal for change will be negative. If the change agent can anticipate this, he will be better prepared to respond to the negative feelings that are expressed. With advance warning he may be able to respond in a manner which will not reinforce these negative feelings, and perhaps he may even be able to help the individual or the group examine the negative reaction in a creative manner.

Third, the more complex the situation or the more complicated the proposal for change, the greater the chance that responses to this may be counterproductive. This initial response tends to be an intuitive one and the intuitive response tends to be counterproductive in complex situations. The immediate response of a university president to call the police when students occupy a building, the opening of the door to the hall by the hotel resident when he learns there is a fire in the building, and the individual's natural inclination to apply the brakes when his car begins to skid on ice are three contemporary examples of an intuitive response to change that is counterproductive.

A fourth point can be traced back to the custom over two thousand years ago to put to death the bearer of bad news. Since many people initially interpret any proposal for change as bad news, it is not surprising that they tend to express hostile feelings not only toward the proposal, but also toward the person who is responsible for introducing the proposal. Again it can be helpful if the change agent sees this as normal human behavior.[16]

Occasionally the advocate of planned change finds his proposal greeted with affirmative and enthusiastic approval the very first time it is presented. If the change agent views this as the normal reaction to an excellent proposal and a thorough presentation, he may be deluding himself. It may be that he has unknowingly presented a proposal that is perceived as a response to a crisis. Since the response to change of both individuals and organizations tends to be significantly different during a crisis than during normal times, it can be very helpful to the change agent if he is aware that he is dealing with a crisis situation.

Finally, the change agent should recognize that a significant factor in the type of reaction he receives to any proposal for change is in his own expectations. There is a vast difference between expecting rejection and being prepared for an initial negative response.

The implications of this summary of people's responses to change can be stated in one sentence. The agent will have fewer frustrations and more successes if he assumes that in the face of change people will behave like normal human beings.

### The Institutional Lag

In 1969 most of the two hundred homes for unwed mothers in the United States had a waiting list. By early

1971 many were faced with a vacancy problem, three in New York announced they were closing, and the Florence Crittenton Association was advertising for clients on a Chicago rock-music radio station.[17] As a result of the decline in the number of persons seeking the services of these homes, many of them are diversifying their program and moving into the care of emotionally disturbed children or other youth-related activities.

The current plight of the home for unwed mothers is only one of many examples that could be cited to illustrate an important aspect of the nature of change. This is the tendency for institutions to continue in the same old pattern long after major societal changes have sharply altered their "market." Whether it is the March of Dimes to eliminate polio, or the church-sponsored college that was chartered to train young men for the ministry but now does not have any pretheological majors in the student body, or the children's home that was founded to care for the orphans of the Civil War dead, the pattern is the same. The passage of time and change have altered or eliminated the original purpose for existence, but the institution tends to continue to attempt to service the old market until it disappears completely, then to seek to identify a new reason for its continued existence.

This pattern of institutional behavior includes three dimensions that are of interest to the change-oriented person.

The lag between societal change and the institutional response is one aspect of the nature of change that soon becomes obvious to every impatient advocate of change. What he can or will do in response to that lag is an entirely different question.

The natural persistence of every institution to continue to function on an earlier set of assumptions that are no longer valid is less obvious, but equally important to the change agent.[18]

The third aspect of this problem is the most subtle, the most neglected, and the most difficult for the change-oriented individual to cope with as he works for planned change. This is the tendency to give simple and obvious explanations that tend to obscure rather than to clarify.

Why is there a decline in the number of persons seeking to use the services of a home for unwed mothers? The answer appears to be perfectly obvious and consists of two parts. Many of the managers of the homes with vacant beds were quick to identify the reason for their current dilemma. The increased distribution and use of birth-control pills is one part of the answer. The recent legalization of abortion in many states is the other part of what is the obvious cause for the decline in the demand for the services of these homes.

The only problem with such an obvious and simple answer is that the number of illegitimate births has increased from 225,000 in 1960 to 318,000 in 1967 to approximately 370,000 in 1970.

Perhaps it is necessary to look more carefully at the reasons for the decline than simply greater use of birth-control pills and the increase in legalized abortions.

Perhaps the type of services these homes have provided the unwed mother in the past no longer are meeting the real needs of the pregnant young girl of the 1970s. Perhaps the mores of society have changed and thus reduced the demand for the private and confidential services of these homes. Perhaps there is a new demand emerging, but these homes have not yet identified it.

Someone may be tempted to say the real reason for the decline in demand is that these homes catered to the white middle-class girl in the past and today the great increase in illegitimate births is among black girls from the lower-income groups, and these girls tend to have and to rear their babies at home.

The only problem with that explanation is that the greatest increase in illegitimate births is among white teenagers. The proportion of all illegitimate children born to Negro mothers has been declining steadily for over fifteen years.

A more careful analysis of the situation suggests that in a relatively short period of time the traditional definition of the need and the traditional definition of the purpose of the traditional maternity homes have become obsolete.

The traditional home for unwed pregnant girls tended to see the "girl-in-trouble" or the "refined" girl who had "made one mistake" as their potential clientele, and the ideological emphasis was on "respectability," "moral reprieve," and "moral reinstatement." The operating procedures stressed secrecy, rigid rules of behavior, and adoption of the baby.[19]

In recent years, however, the presuppositions on which the help offered the unwed pregnant girls is based have changed sharply. Today there is a widespread assumption among professional social workers that the illegitimate pregnancy is psychologically motivated. As a result, the purpose of the "new style" homes has changed from moral reprieve to helping the girls discover and understand the psychological reasons behind their predicament. Instead of providing an extraordinarily protective atmosphere which helped the girl deny her own responsibility for the situation, the emphasis is now on helping the girl accept responsibility for the pregnancy and for what she is.

Perhaps even more significant is the change in the manner in which society views the unwed pregnant girl and the manner in which she views herself. A simple illustration of this is the code of behavior in high schools. In 1960 it was very unusual for a high school to allow an obviously pregnant girl to attend classes. By 1970 it was relatively common, and several public school districts saw the continued care and education of the pregnant teenager as a part of their normal responsibility.

The response of an institution to change, the tendency to continue to operate on an increasingly obsolete set of assumptions, the tendency to offer simple explanations for complex changes, and the tendency to continue to "push its old product" rather than change to meet a new definition of need is illustrated very clearly by the empty beds in many of today's maternity homes.

These same characteristics of institutional lag as a part of the nature of change also can be seen in the current dilemma of many service clubs and lodges, in the thousands of empty Sunday school classrooms scattered across the nation, in the closings every day of scores of family grocery stores and pharmacies, in the disappearance of over one thousand family farms every week, and in the death of several relatively young community organizations every day.

## The Influence of a Crisis

The major exceptions to much that has been written earlier in this chapter can be gathered together under the word "crisis." Change in the face of a *perceived* crisis tends to arouse a different set of responses in people and to be carried out with a different set of ground rules.

By definition, a crisis is an unstable time or a crucial period in the state of affairs of an individual or a group. Not infrequently there is a lag between the time when the period of crisis actually begins and when it is perceived. Until it is perceived, the behavioral responses will tend to follow the normal patterns. It also is important to note that often people perceive a crisis long before they are prepared to admit its existence. This means that one of the first responsibilities of an agent of change is to help people articulate the existence of a crisis which they have perceived but have not been ready to openly recognize.

In the time of a perceived crisis it eventually becomes apparent to most people that the cost of inaction is greater than the cost of action. One of the responsibilities of an agent of change is to help people come to that realization sooner. Likewise, during a crisis the failure of any one group to act tends to have a high degree of visibility to other groups and the costs of this inaction tend also to be highly visible. One result is that a crisis tends to reverse the normal roles in a change situation. During a crisis the influence of the proponents of change is increased, the opponents of change are on the defensive as the normal anti-change biases of society are set aside temporarily, and the whole process is accelerated.[20]

Russell Dynes has suggested that during a disaster, which is one form of a crisis, an organization often very quickly gains control over the allocation of resources it previously did not control, and new priorities are developed and accepted for the allocation of these resources. These resources include manpower, economic resources, and loyalty. A disaster also often produces the development of an "emergency consensus" in the decision-making process.[21]

A crisis also tends to open up the channels of communication, to accelerate the speed of communications, to facilitate the opportunities for two-way communication, to substantially alter the behavior of individuals, to allow decisions to be made at a lower level than is normally acceptable, to provide opportunities for the reduction of conflicts among groups or organizations, and to reduce the chances the victim will be blamed for his situation.[22]

Since a crisis, even when of less than disaster proportions, alters the rules of the game of planned change, it behooves the advocate of planned change to be conscious of this. Most people intuitively know that a crisis alters the normal reaction to change. For this reason some impatient advocates of change carry a can of gasoline to pour on the coals of discontent whenever they find themselves in a situation where the reactions to their proposals for change vary from apathy to opposition. The other side of this picture is that people also intuitively tend to be able to distinguish between a real crisis and an artificial one.

While the impact of a crisis on the normal responses to change should not be overlooked, a mastery of the crisis theory of change is less useful than an understanding of the process of planned social change.

# 3

# The Process of Planned Change

On Monday, May 3, 1971, an estimated 50,000 war protesters attempted to "shut down the government" by blocking the roads and bridges leading into Washington, D.C. By eight o'clock that morning the police had most of the streets open for traffic and absenteeism in federal offices was reported to be below normal for a Monday morning.

Two weeks later 13,000 railroad signalmen went on strike for a pay increase. By Tuesday morning they had cut off the transportation for 300,000 commuters, halted all freight shipments across the nation, and steel plants were making plans to curtail production. It was predicted that if the strike continued throughout the week, millions of workers would be laid off as the nation's production and distribution systems would be crippled by the strike. By Tuesday afternoon it was clear that the Congress felt obligated to intervene and grant the workers a raise, thus ending the strike.

These two incidents illustrate several of the basic principles that are a part of the change process.

One of the most obvious is the value of organization and allies, or what is often referred to as a supporting group. The railroad signalmen had a very powerful supporting group in the half-million rail employees who honored their picket lines.

These two episodes also illustrate the general principle that in any society there is far more acceptance for efforts directed at change that are channeled through the established avenues for protest. Today a labor strike usually is accepted as a legal, although frequently highly unpopular, vehicle for protest of the status quo. Blocking the flow of vehicular traffic on the highways in one metropolitan area during rush hour, although far less disruptive of living patterns or of the nation's economy than a railroad strike, is not yet a socially acceptable means of protest in the United States. It should be noted that this is a conditional statement reflecting the values and attitudes of the American population at a given point in history. Thirty-five years ago a strike was a far less acceptable form of behavior than it was in 1971. Perhaps in 1988 blocking highway traffic during rush hour will be a socially acceptable form of behavior.

Anyone interested in the subject of change should recognize that the public response has a tremendous influence on behavioral patterns. A highly visible recent example of this is the recent tremendous increase in the number of Roman Catholic nuns and priests leaving the religious life.

This change in vocations has been facilitated by the change in the response of the American population. A few years ago such a change was greeted by strong public disapproval. Today the public response tends to range from neutral to favorable.

Closely related to this point on the response of the general public is the distinction between what might be described as a "prophetic witness" directed at changing the climate of public opinion and efforts that are directed primarily or solely at change. There are substantial reasons to believe that many of the persons engaged in the war protest in Washington were primarily, if not entirely, concerned with making a public witness to their desire for peace. It is doubtful if they actually believed their actions would result directly in the withdrawal of American troops from Vietnam. By contrast the railroad signalmen probably had little interest in changing the public's attitude toward the wages paid railroad employees. They were almost entirely concerned about changing the level of their own compensation.

When placed next to each other, these two incidents also offer a lesson on strategy and tactics. The change-oriented individual or group with a strategy which emphasizes change rather than witness tends to choose socially acceptable channels of protest, or to work through the established procedures for decision-making, or to "work within the system," to use a cliché of the era. Thus the opponents of the Vietnam war, who were pursuing a strategy emphasizing a dramatic public witness, worked outside the system by attempting to "shut down the government." At the same time another group of opponents of the war were pursuing a strategy of change which called for cutting off the Congressional appropriations that financed the United States intervention in Vietnam. Their tactics were directed at securing enough votes to win that fight on the floor of the Senate. They were not attempting to make a public witness; they were concerned primarily and directly with change, and this led them to choose to work within the system or "the club," as the United States Senate is sometimes described.

Two weeks later, after nineteen months of negotiations had failed, the railroad signalmen escalated their effort at change by going out on strike.

## Force Field Analysis

Another concept in the process of social change that is illustrated by these incidents is the "force field analysis" approach to planned change. This model originated with Kurt Lewin and is widely used.[1] Lewin suggested that change can be viewed as a result of the shifting of the balance of forces that are working in opposite directions and maintaining a dynamic equilibrium or the status quo. This balance can be altered by increasing the forces that are exerting pressure on one side, by reducing the pressures of the forces on the other side, or by a combination of the two.

The protesters against the war were seeking to achieve change by increasing the pressure on the Aministration from the peace or dove side of the hawk-dove balance. At the same time a number of senators were seeking to reduce the resistance among some of their colleagues to a proposal to cut the appropriations that were financing a continuation of the war.

Likewise, this model can be applied to the rail strike where the signalmen were attempting to secure a change in their compensation by increasing the pressure on one side of this balance of forces. The intervention of the Congress provided the additional pressure on that side of the stalemate that was necessary to move their wage scale to a higher level.

In most situations change is a result of a combination of forces. An excellent recent example of this has been the opening of new employment opportunities to Negroes. Significant progress in correcting this centuries-old form of injustice to blacks was achieved only when efforts were made to reduce the pressures for continued racial discrimination on one side of this balance of power and were accompanied by an increase in the pressures for equal rights on the other side of the equation. While this is somewhat of an oversimplification of a very complex subject, change occurred as a result of the contributions of *both* those who were making a highly visible public witness against discrimination on one side and those who were concentrating on the actual details or mechanics of change on the other side. The former tended to be viewed as "outsiders" who were protesting the status quo and thus increasing the pressure for change. The latter tended to be viewed as "insiders" who were reducing the pressure of the forces that kept blacks from being employed in a great variety of jobs or barred the door to Negroes seeking admission to medical school or restricted their opportunities for voting and holding public office.

Lewin's model is a very useful one for the change-oriented person and it illustrates again the value of alliances. These alliances often can include not only those who are working to change the amount of pressure on one side of this equation, but also those who are interested in working to change the pressure on the other side.

Unfortunately, however, change-oriented individuals have a tendency to "choose up sides" in a very unsophisticated manner. Again using Lewin's model, anyone on the "other side" often is viewed as an enemy rather than as a potential ally—"Anyone who is not with us (on our side of Lewin's model of a balance of opposing forces) is against us."

The possibility of building an alliance between like-minded persons from the two sides of a balance of forces can be seen somewhat more clearly in looking at the analysis of intentional social change that has been suggested by Alvin Pitcher. His basic theory consists of two elements, "you have to push from the bottom and persuade at the top." [2] Pitcher emphasizes that unless there is a strong push from the bottom, the efforts at persuasion at the top probably will not produce much in terms of change.

Reflection on Pitcher's theory helps explain why planned social change usually requires at least two styles of leadership, the "insider" who persuades, often with a low degree of visibility, and the "outsider" who pushes, often with a very high degree of visibility. When these two types of change-oriented leaders can each see the other as an ally, the pace of change often can be accelerated and the direction controlled more effectively.

While not incompatible with Lewin's model of a dynamic balance of forces, there is another approach to the subject of planned change that enables a person to see even more clearly the crucial importance of allies. It is illustrated by one of the most dramatic political struggles in recent American constitutional history.

## The Process of Planned Change

The first major defeat handed President Franklin D. Roosevelt by the Congress was the rejection in 1937 of his proposal to increase the number of justices on the Supreme Court from nine to fifteen. The plan of action he followed was an adaptation of one originally conceived by James C. McReynolds back in 1913 when he was Woodrow Wilson's attorney general. In 1937, ironically, McReynolds was the most consistently anti–New Deal of any of the four conservative justices on the Court who repeatedly had acted to declare New Deal legislation unconstitutional.

In a review of the events of that 168-day battle that ended with recommittal of the President's bill, five tactical errors stand out that illustrate critical factors in the process of planned change.

The first mistake made by Roosevelt was in overestimating the extent of the discontent with the conservative attitude of the Supreme Court. His second error was in neglecting to develop a larger initiating group. He had never mentioned the issue during the 1936 presidential campaign and he sent his plan for reorganizing the judiciary to Congress without any consultation of or even warning to his congressional leaders. The basic initiating group consisted only of the President and Attorney General Homer Cummings. Most of the other members of the cabinet knew nothing of the proposal until it had been announced publicly.

Roosevelt's third tactical error was his failure to build up a supporting group on behalf of his plan. Closely related was his fourth mistake. Instead of developing either a proposal that had a clear tone of legitimacy or one for which a case could be built, he proposed a plan which appeared to threaten the life of one of the nation's sacred institutions.

Finally, the President's tactics and strategy were incompatible. His strategy called for a Supreme Court that would be more amenable to change and to new legislative approaches. For this he had many open or potential allies. The tactics used by the President, however, were based on the limitations that accompany old age. By openly questioning the capacity of anyone who had passed his seventieth birthday, the President aroused the ire of the friends of eighty-year-old Justice Louis Brandeis, who had been one of Roosevelt's most consistent supporters. Even more critical, this was not the most creative method of enlisting allies in the Congress, where the rule of seniority meant that most or all of the influential leaders either had passed or were approaching their seventieth birthday.

Whether he carries the title of president, politician, pastor, or pacifist, the change agent must understand the basic elements of the process of planned or intentional change to be effective. There have been countless efforts to break the process down into a series of steps, and there is a remarkable degree of consistency among most of these statements. As the change agent seeks to develop his own style or methodology, he can profit by looking at several of these.

One of the simplest and one of the most influential was formulated by Kurt Lewin.[3] In an article published in 1943, he wrote that a successful effort at change in either individual or group performance consists of three steps:

1. Unfreeze the present situation.
2. Move to a new level.
3. Freeze the group life at the new level.

In this essay he pointed out that his experiences had led him to believe that any change toward a higher level of performance tended to be short-lived, since there was a natural tendency to slip back to the old level.

A nineteenth-century evangelist might look at this conceptualization of the process of change and ask, "What else is new? This outlines our task as evangelists. First we help a person to realize he is a sinner. That 'unfreezes' the situation. Next he is converted, and third he makes a commitment that 'freezes' him as a reborn person. Without a solid commitment he may backslide."

A decade later, Ronald Lippitt and others expanded Lewin's concept into a five-phase process built around the role of the change agent.[4] This begins with the "unfreezing" of the present situation as the need for change is perceived, moves to the establishment of a relationship built around change, the effort to change the situation, the "freezing" of the new set of circumstances, and the termination of the relationship of the change agent to the situation.

Lippitt and his colleagues also suggested that the third step in this process, what Lewin termed "moving to the new level," could be divided into three phases. These consist of definition of the problem, review of alternative courses of action, and the transformation of the goals into actual accomplishment.[5]

Seifert and Clinebell, as they focused on the role of the indigenous church leader as an agent of change in contrast to Lippitt's approach which emphasized the role of the outsider or consultant, have suggested a five-step process. This consists of (1) motivation and preparation, (2) diagnosis of the problem and consideration of alternative courses of action, (3) the formulation of a strategy and of day-to-day tactics, (4) carrying out the plan of action, and finally (5) review, evaluation, and the stabilization of change.[6]

This is a useful frame of reference, combining a simple definition of the planning process with Lewin's model to produce a more action-oriented outline than is represented by the typical definition of the planning process.

One of the most elaborate and detailed descriptive analyses of social change has been developed by George Beal and his associates at Iowa State University.[7] This fifteen-step outline provides an instructive framework for looking at specific situations. Since it is a rare individual who is able to walk around carrying a fifteen-step action model in his head, this model has its greatest value as an analytical tool and is of limited value for operational purposes.

Specialists in community development have much to contribute to this discussion of steps involved in the process of planned change. An example of this is the analytical model prepared by Marshall B. Clinard in a slum area in India. His model consists of seven stages:

1. Early reactions to the program
2. Stimulating the idea of self-help

3. Search for indigenous leadership
4. Developing new leadership
5. Establishing legitimation
6. The organization and action phase
7. Development of a new self-image.[8]

These five models of the process of planned social change are sufficient to emphasize the importance of two basic considerations for the change agent. The more obvious is that no single definition of the process fits perfectly for every situation and every individual. More important is the need for each individual to pick out and adapt to his own situation the model that meets his needs and fits his personality.

The perspective, personality, and role of the person who is involved in the change process will influence both his perception of the process and his evaluation of the usefulness of various models. The action-oriented individual who is deeply involved in the process of planned change probably will pick a different model of the process than will the person who, from an academic perspective, is analyzing what happened in the past. The indigenous leader probably will be more comfortable and effective with a model different from that used by the outsider or the consultant. The community organizer probably will find one model adapts very comfortably to his own personality and style of operation while the community developer may choose a different model.

An extremely useful operational definition of the process of planned social change that combines both the descriptive and the analytical has been developed by Christopher

Sower and his colleagues. Their five-stage model can be presented in a form that the change-oriented individual can use both for his own guidance and for analyzing the efforts of others. This model consists of these steps:

1. Convergence of interest (discontent with the status quo)
2. Establishment of an initiating set
3. Legitimation and sponsorship (the development of a supporting group)
4. Establishment of an execution set and mobilization of community resources
5. Fulfillment of "charter" (freezing at the new level of performance)[9]

This five-phase model not only incorporates the "unfreeze-change-freeze" concept of Lewin's; it presents the process in a form that can be used as a checklist by the action-oriented individual as he plans for change. In addition, it can be used as an outline for examining the change process in more detail.

## The Importance of Discontent

In any discussion of intentional change it is almost impossible to overstate the importance of discontent. Without discontent with the present situation there can be no planned, internally motivated and directed intentional change. This does *not* mean that there will be no change, for there will be many changes. The changes that do occur, however, will be the result of a crisis, of external forces, or of an accident. (See Chapter 2 for a more detailed discussion of the sources of change.) Without discontent there will be no intentional change originating from within that social structure, regardless of whether the social structure under consideration is a neighborhood, a school, a unit of government, a business, a church, or a voluntary association.

Thus the first question for the change-oriented individual is a simple one: "Is anyone else dissatisfied with the present situation?" If the answer is in the negative, the door to intentional planned change is closed. There are, however, many ways to open that door, and often that is the first task of the agent of change.[10]

Saul Alinsky has made famous one prescription for that step. His phrase "rub raw the sores of discontent" has become a battle cry for many change-oriented persons.[11] This is a simple, clear, and colorful description of one approach to increasing both the extent and the depth of discontent with the status quo. Before looking at other approaches to increasing the degree of discontent, it may be helpful to look at the first major pitfall that a change agent may encounter in the process of planned change.

In every effort to enlarge the degree of discontent there is a risk that the effort may be counterproductive. Dr. Walter Menninger, coordinator of development for the Menninger Foundation and a member of President Johnson's National Commission on the Causes and Prevention of Violence, pointed this out in a discussion of the Walker Report on the disorders in Chicago during the 1968 Democratic Convention. While he said he did not disagree with the facts in the report—which few read—he did disagree with the manner in which the conclusions were presented in the widely read summary. He said use of the term "police riot" made many people reject the findings of the Walker committee.[12] If the goal is to increase the degree of discontent and to polarize a community, the language can, and perhaps should, be offensive. If, however, the goal is to increase the level of discontent as an essential preliminary step in the process of planned change, certain tactics, including the language chosen, require more thoughtful consideration. An essential element in the process of planned change is the mobilization of a support group or the building of an organization. The wrong choice of tactics can impede that part of the process.

This point can be illustrated by the tactics of the Students for a Democratic Society (SDS) and tactics of a change-oriented community organizer. In recent years SDS has become largely a revolutionary organization and their tactics, which call for increasing the degree of polarization in the nation, while perhaps a bit naïve in many respects, are consistent with a revolutionary strategy—and revolution is the avowed goal of at least one or two of the many splinter groups that have been an outgrowth of the original movement.

By contrast, the change-oriented community organizer recognizes that to be effective discontent must be channeled into the problem-solving process in respect to specific problems.[13] If the tactics, including the language used in arousing discontent, are viewed as offensive by many people, this may become a major obstacle in subsequent steps of the process.[14]

Another approach to this subject of discontent as the initial step in the change process is to turn to four of the basic sources of discontent.

The first is the response to a bad decision, or at least what is perceived as a bad decision. Many social movements which ultimately become the initiators of change are first organized around the discontent that is a part of the response to what is perceived as a bad decision. Examples of this are the Populist movement of the late nineteenth century which owed much of its strength to decisions by the railroads that were perceived as bad for farmers, the rise of labor unions, the response to President Roosevelt's decision to "pack" the Supreme Court, the political support garnered by George Wallace in his 1968 candidacy for the presidency, Martin Luther's role in the Protestant Reformation, the creation of the National Association of Congregational Christian Churches as a result of the merger of the Evangelical and Reformed Church with the Congregational Christian Church to form the United Church of Christ, the response of the nation to the televised tactics used by Bull Connor and other police officers in Selma, Alabama, in 1967, the withdrawal of President Lyndon B. Johnson from the 1968 presidential contest, and the creation of literally hundreds of community organizations to oppose urban renewal proposals or plans for new freeways.

In each of these a decision or action by someone else was perceived as a bad decision and the resulting discontent was sufficiently large to produce significant changes.

A second and related means of creating another source of discontent with the status quo is to deliberately cause a malfunction in one of the accepted means of social control.[15] The most common recent example of this has been the efforts of some participants in several demonstrations to provoke the police to excessive retaliatory responses, an action which it is hoped will "radicalize" both the non-violent protesters and the spectators. Another example has been the threat by several Roman Catholic leaders in some communities to close their parochial schools, thus flooding the public schools with an unexpectedly large and sudden increase in enrollment, unless financial aid is granted to parochial schools. It is expected this threat will cause many non-Catholics to press for a change in the laws which bar the use of public funds for the support of parochial schools. Still another application of this approach to expanding discontent with the status quo is to encourage rigid enforcement of an unwanted law in the expectation that this will arouse enough discontent to secure repeal or at least an amendment of the law.

A third approach to raising the level of discontent is sometimes referred to as the "vision and model" concept. In this a person is enabled to see both a vision of what could be and also a working model of how that vision or dream could be turned into reality.[16]

One of the most common contemporary illustrations of the application of this concept is the demonstration project or pilot program. This technique has been used by county agricultural agents, 4-H club leaders, Peace Corps workers, leaders in teacher-training programs, civil rights leaders, antipoverty programs, and State Department–sponsored tours of foreign businessmen, teachers, and community leaders to the United States.

There is a fourth approach to creating discontent, however, which overlaps all three of these other approaches and which can be described as the basic source of discontent. This is discovery by an individual for himself of the difference between the ideal and reality. It stands out by itself as a subject deserving separate consideration by every agent of change.

## The Self-Identified Discrepancy

Three white business executives and a staff person from the National Association for the Advancement of Colored People were talking with a thirty-five-year-old Negro mother in the living room of her home in the Hough area of Cleveland. The NAACP had planned a Saturday morning tour for white business leaders to give them a firsthand view of the housing available to black people. As they chatted, the three white businessmen kept moving in the direction of the kitchen. They wanted to see all three rooms on the first floor of this small frame house. While she was very polite, they received no encouragement from the housewife. Eventually, however, they had edged over until two of them were standing in the doorway between the living room and the kitchen. Suddenly water began to flood down through the ceiling and doused one of the men.

"What in the world is this?" he exclaimed as he jumped out of the way and dabbed at the spots on his $200 suit with his handkerchief.

"Oh my goodness! I was afraid that might happen," replied the housewife. "You see, every time the people upstairs flush the toilet it overflows and runs down through the ceiling."

"Well, why don't you complain and get the landlord to fix it?" he asked impatiently.

"Oh, we've tried that," she replied, "but he just says that if we don't like it here we can move, and we don't have any other place to go."

As he drove home later that Saturday morning to his $70,000 home in the suburbs, this business executive in the damp suit decided the time had come for him and his company to become involved in helping to solve the housing problem of Cleveland's black residents.

"Your assignment is to design a tough white-racist social and economic system without any loopholes for the Negro to escape from the racial, social, and economic trap he has been caught in for the past three hundred years," said the social studies teacher to his class in "New Perspectives in Race" in a suburban Detroit school. "This system you are designing must apply to both rural and urban America, to both the central city and the suburbs, and to both the educated and the uneducated black person!"

When the class finishes this assignment, the students are asked to compare this racist system they have deliberately designed with the social system that actually exists in the United States.

"In a situation such as ours, can a church be both Christian and Lutheran?" This question was raised by the pastor of an all-white Lutheran Church—Missouri Synod congregation in a racially changing neighborhood.

"Hopefully there is at least some degree of overlap," was the reply.

"You're missing the point," responded the pastor. "Is it realistic to expect that a congregation with the strong German traditions we have to be able to reach out and minister to people from a completely different cultural background.

It seems to me that we have only two choices. Either we remain Lutheran and deny our Christian evangelistic responses or we act as a Christian congregation and lose our Lutheran heritage."

Each of these three incidents represents the application of the concept of the self-identified discrepancy with a resulting increase in the level of discontent with the status quo.

The drenched Cleveland businessman experienced first-hand the discrepancy between the quality of housing in the black ghetto and white suburbia. The social studies class saw there was little difference between the tough racist social system they had invented and reality—but a great discrepancy between both of those and the American dream. The Lutheran pastor saw the discrepancy between the cultural and ethnic traditions of his church and the Christian call to evangelism.

The self-identified discrepancy breeds discontent in the businessman who compares this year's profits with higher figures for each of the past five years; in the nineteen-year-old who contrasts the current American foreign policy with the ideals he had been taught in school; in the African student of a Christian missionary school who compares the teachings of the New Testament and of the American Declaration of Independence with conditions in his land; in the young people who wrote the preamble to the report of the 1971 White House Conference on Youth and contrasted the high ideals on which this nation was founded with the current privation, fear, and sense of repression; in the president of the theological seminary who remembers when the accrediting association was viewed as an ally and now finds himself an unwilling servant of that association; in the teen-ager who hears adults insisting that the manufacture, sale, and use of alcoholic beverages is legal but the mere possession of marijuana is a crime; in the sixty-six-year-old man who looks at his $110 Social Security check as he watches the televised report of a student rebellion at a university where it costs $4,000 a year to attend; and in the laymen who see the average attendance drop by 40 percent in the first year of the new pastor's tenure.

The self-identified discrepancy is a part of the response to what is perceived as a "bad" decision, to the decision behind the effort to cause a malfunction in the social control system and in the vision and model approach to planned change.

Another way of looking at the concept of the self-identified discrepancy is to contrast it with a very common approach to change. This is for an "outsider" to identify for members of a group the discrepancy between their current situation and the ideal. While this is not a completely useless approach, it is far less effective than enabling people to discover the discrepancy for themselves. This includes enabling others to both define the ideal and to discover the difference between that ideal and their current situation.

A widely used approach to this has been the self-study process which typically was designed to assist the members of an organization to describe their present situation, to develop an ideal, and to identify the discrepancy between the two. Many of these self-study programs failed when the process became an end in itself rather than a means to an end.

Another approach is the survey to determine the discrepancy between the ideal and reality. In April, 1968, for example, the Minneapolis Urban Coalition and the Minnesota Council on Religion and Race jointly sponsored a questionnaire that was filled out by 67,000 churchgoers. The questionnaire was directed at discovering the attitudes of whites on racial issues. It was planned on the premise that the results of the survey would spur efforts at educational programs to help change white persons' understanding of black leadership and black self-determination. Once people can see the discrepancy between the ideal and reality, the door is open for educational programs to make a difference.

For the change agent, the concept of the self-identified discrepancy is one of his half-dozen most valuable tools as he goes about his business of initiating and facilitating the process of planned change. As he uses this tool, however, he should recognize that it is vulnerable to a variety of malfunctions. As mentioned earlier, the process used may become an end in itself or it may so exhaust the energies of people that they are not interested in going beyond this first step in the change process.

There is also the risk that the agent of change may become so wrapped up in raising the level of discontent that he fails to see the necessity either for forming an initiating group or for building a supporting group.

## The Initiating Group

The second phase of the process of planned change is the formation of the initiating group. There is a vast difference between sitting around complaining about the current situation and actually beginning to do something about it. This is the difference between the first and second steps in the process of planned change. It is also the first point at which the process may break down. The number of persons who find it easy to complain about contemporary conditions is far greater than the number who are willing to share in efforts to introduce change. One result of this is that the agent of change often finds it easier—and frequently more enjoyable—to work at increasing the degree of discontent than to organize the necessary initiating group.

Occasionally the initiating group consists of a single individual. Rosa Parks, the lady who refused to move to the back of a Birmingham bus in December of 1955; Ralph Nader, the crusader for consumers' rights; Jerry Mander, the advertising executive and conservationist who popularized the idea of the coupon to be clipped from a newspaper advertisement and mailed to a public official; and Senator Eugene McCarthy are four recent examples of what *began* as one-person initiating groups. Each was discontented and each initiated a plan of action for change. In each case, however, this initiating group soon was enlarged.

During the first stage of the process of planned change, the rise in the level of discontent, the problem is identified by an increasing number of persons.

During the second stage of the process, the problem is defined more sharply, the forces that are causing or perpetuating the problem are identified, and a strategy is devised to change the situation. In working through this second phase it may be helpful for the agent of change to prepare a checklist for himself. While each person will include the items that fit his own unique situation, these six items may provide a basis for developing a checklist.

The first item could be Kurt Lewin's force field model for identifying the driving forces and the restraining forces that maintain or cause the present difficulty. Should the strategy be to increase the pressure on one side of the present balance of forces or to reduce the pressure on the other side? Or both?

While Lewin's model is not the only one that can be used in diagnosing the points of intervention and distinguishing symptoms from problems, it does have several advantages. One of the most useful characteristics of the force field analysis is that it builds into the process of analysis the expectation that there are *at least* two solutions to every problem.

Out of this analysis will naturally come the formulation of a tentative strategy, or more often a series of alternative strategies, for changing the situation. These should be examined not only in terms of their probable impact on the present situation, but also for the probable consequences of each one.

This leads to the third item on the checklist, the subject of price tags. Every proposal for a change from the status quo has a price tag on it. This price tag normally is the sum of two costs. The first, and most obvious, is the cost in resources (time, energy, loyalties, money, skills, etc.) that will be required to implement a strategy of change. The second, and a frequently neglected cost, is the consequences of any change from the status quo. Sometimes these indirect costs outweigh the direct costs, in terms of the resources necessary to achieve the change.

Examples of the costs that are a part of the consequences include the displacement of millions of marginal farm families by changes in agricultural technology, the impact on mass transit systems of the construction of freeways into the large central cities, and the increased air pollution resulting from the addition of lead to gasoline. In each case the indirect costs of the consequences turned out to be greater than the direct costs of the change.

Another item on the checklist is the question of motivation. The change agent should examine his own motives, and he also will find it helpful to inquire about the motivation of others. The greater his self-awareness of his own goals, motives, values, and needs, the more likely it is that he will be able to be helpful to the persons he is working with throughout the change process.

A fifth item on the checklist is the need and method for stablizing the changes once they have been accomplished. The first question here is whether or not the change should be made permanent. Often this is not necessary, and it even may be undesirable. For example, for years five neighboring congregations have been holding separate Thanksgiving services. They may decide to have one joint service next November. This change from the traditional pattern may need to be institutionalized and made permanent. It may not. A professional boxer may need to get his weight down to 175 pounds for one match. It may be unwise for him to "freeze" this reduction in his weight.

The other side of this issue is that in many efforts at change it is desirable to freeze the new changed set of circumstances. The means of doing this should be included in this second step of the process of planned change.

101

The last item on this checklist is the "re-entry problem." While it does not exist in every case of planned change, it is sufficiently common to deserve special attention.

Frequently the identification of discontent occurs when a few members of an organization or community are gathered together apart from the others. This often leads not only to an increase in the level of discontent, but also to the formation of an initiating group which develops a plan of action. This may occur while this small group of persons is attending a meeting or involved in a training program away from home. The most common basis for the emergence of this group, which has its own clearly defined ideas on what must be done, is the committee or task force appointed to study future alternatives. When the individuals return to the larger group, there is a tendency for them to identify themselves, and to be identified by others, as a separate cadre who have their own distinctive view of what needs to be done and how to do it.

Instead of seeing themselves or the experience they have shared as the source of this "elite phenomenon," they have a tendency to blame the members of the larger group for not understanding the problem, for being too apathetic, for being too closely wedded to the status quo, or for not being ready to act on the course of action proposed by the cadre.

Unless the re-entry problem is recognized, there is the ever present danger that the initiating group may become a cadre of people who are alienated from the rest of the members of the organization. Among other consequences, this means their capability to function as a force for change will be sharply reduced.

While there is no single simple answer to this problem,

there are several ways of reducing the stalemate that occurs when an initiating group becomes identified as an elite outgroup by the other members of the organization. One way is to keep enlarging the initiating group with new participants from the rest of the larger group. Another is for the initiating group to see itself as seeking change to solve a problem rather than as the originators of the single, perfect, rigid, and only applicable solution to the problem or source of discontent. A third is to avoid the tactics, including language, that may foster hostility and rejection from the larger group. A fourth is to understand the process of introducing a new idea into an organization and the rejection that normally greets the appearance of a new idea.[17] Most important of all, however, is the process by which members of the initiating group attempt to view their proposal and their own actions from the perspective of the other members of the organization who have not been a part of the change process to this stage. Finally, it usually is wise not to spend too much time on the formation and work of the initiating group and to move on to the creation of the larger and more inclusive supporting group.

## The Supporting Group

On August 10, 1970, the proposed constitutional amendment guaranteeing equal rights for women passed the House of Representatives by a 352-15 vote. Since eighty-three members of the United States Senate were soon to sign up as co-sponsors of the amendment, it appeared to many observers that it would sail through the Senate with far more than the required two-thirds majority.

The amendment never actually reached the point of being voted on in the Senate.[18]

What happened?

In simple language, the women supporting this constitutional amendment built up a strong supporting group in the House of Representatives, where Mrs. Martha Griffiths, one of the ten women members of the House, was a powerful ally. The combination of Mrs. Griffiths and an election year was more than sufficient to cancel out the opposition of Representative Emanuel Celler and his Judiciary Committee. (For forty-seven years this committee had been sitting on a proposed amendment granting equal rights to women.)

The amendment did not have the backing of a strong supporting group in the Senate, however, and the opponents were able to keep it from coming to a floor vote.

This incident illustrates six of the essential elements that are present in an effective supporting group. The first is numbers. While there were 83 senators who were publicly committed to this amendment, they were not supported (pressured) by a large bloc of voters who were watching closely to make sure they honored this commitment. In the key Senate vote, which was on an amendment to exempt women from the military draft, 27 of the 83 voted for the amendment. This was the same as voting to reject the House version and thus a subtle means of saying to the Senate leaders that the amendment could not get the required two-thirds majority.

The second essential element of an effective supporting group is the capability to legitimatize a proposed change. This "stamp of approval" often is essential to gain certain other required support. It can take many forms. In this case the approval of Senator Sam Ervin of the Senate Judiciary Committee was required to legitimatize the proposal. Without his approval, or at least his neutrality, the amendment could be attacked on the grounds that it was unnecessary and that, as Senator Birch Bayh declared, "The most important reason for enacting this amendment is its symbolic value." If it had had the stamp of approval of Senator Ervin, constitutional conservative, the amendment probably would have secured the necessary two-thirds vote in the Senate. The leading formal sponsor of the amendment in the Senate was Eugene McCarthy, and by September, 1970, he had neither the interest nor the capability necessary to legitimatize an issue such as this.

It is difficult to overemphasize the value of providing legitimacy for any proposal for change. The means of doing this vary tremendously. In Illinois in early 1971 the supporters of a bill in the state legislature that would legalize bingo adopted the slogan "Keep Grandma off the streets," and most of the proponents of the bill at the public hearing were either grandmothers or priests.

A few days before the incident described in the opening paragraph of this chapter, a group of veterans protesting the war in Vietnam gave a sense of legitimacy to their protest by tossing their medals over a fence at a certain point in the parade route. This action, combined with their status as veterans and the eloquent plea of John Kerry, gave a sense of legitimacy to their protest and thus helped win public sympathy, if not approval, for their plea for a change in American foreign policy. This tone of legitimacy was missing from the subsequent protest of the May Day tribe.

A few years ago a group of inner city residents in

Indianapolis, led by a couple of ministers, were protesting the proposed route and construction of a freeway through that part of the city. They were regarded as a relatively unimportant group of troublemakers until the Methodist bishop in Indiana agreed to send a telegram to the governor, asking for a moratorium on all freeway construction in the city until certain policy questions were resolved. When he made public this message, it immediately legitimatized the effort to change the old policies.

Among the most common efforts to legitimatize an issue are the use of well-known and prestigious names on a letterhead, the honorary chairman, the editorial in the newspaper, the open support of important decision-makers, the newspaper advertisement filled with the names of individuals, and the creation of special single-purpose supporting organizations.

A third essential element in the building of a supporting group is loyalty. The importance of loyalty is sometimes overlooked in the efforts to develop a supporting group. Its value is most visible in its absence. One of the most significant dimensions of this resource becomes apparent when the invitation or the desire to join a newly emerging effort directed at change produces a conflict in loyalties. A clear and highly visible example of this could be seen in the 1968 efforts of Eugene McCarthy to develop an antiwar coalition. This produced a conflict of loyalty in several individuals who felt a strong sense of loyalty toward either Lyndon B. Johnson or Robert F. Kennedy, but who also were very sympathetic with McCarthy's position.

Another essential ingredient in an effective supporting group is skill or expertise, and especially the combination of dedication and skill. This skilled leadership is necessary first to gain the necessary approval or adoption of the proposed change and, second, to make the change an operational reality. The group supporting the women's rights amendment had this kind of leadership in the House of Representatives in Mrs. Griffiths. They did not have it in the Senate—and they lost there.

The skills necessary will vary with the type of change that is under consideration and with the procedures, but in most efforts at planned change skill in developing an organization is important, if not critical, at this stage of the process.

Perhaps even more important than organizational expertise, is a skill in the legal field and in legislation. Today, more than ever before in American history, the legal process is being used as an avenue to secure change. The legal system and the courts are being used increasingly both to achieve change and to block efforts at change. Recent examples are the use of the courts to halt pollution of the environment, to block construction of the Cross-Florida Barge Canal, to change the welfare system, and to hasten the removal of ineffective drugs from the market. Harvard Law School professor Louis L. Jaffe estimated that the number of public-action suits on the federal level increased 150 times between 1966 and 1971.[19] It is unlikely that the importance of the legal system and the courts as a channel for planned social change will diminish during the next two decades, regardless of whom the President may appoint to the United States Supreme Court.

It is also probable that the future will see a continuation in the growing demand for a combination of skills in which law is one of the components. Law and accounting, law and medicine, law and engineering, law and planning, and law and social work are some of the contemporary illustrations of this pairing of skills. Law and theology is one of the latest additions to this list.

Another skill which is extremely important both in the total change process and in the building of a support group is competence in communications. People do believe what they are told. While it might be highly desirable, and perhaps also very disrupting, if people were more critical and more skeptical, the fact remains that people do believe what they read in the newspapers, magazines, and books and what they see and hear on radio and television. While some of what is presented is not true, and much is only a part of the truth, the tendency is for people to believe what they read, see, and hear. Repetition increases credibility.

The most highly visible evidence of this characteristic of American society is commercial advertising. The change agent who attempts to build a supporting group today and ignores the importance of skilled communication either is naïve or has a martyr complex.

A fifth element that often is an essential element of an effective supporting group is expressed in the concept of a coalition. This is a substantially different concept than the one reflected in sheer numbers. Whether for better or for worse, the decision-making process in American society in this century has been dominated by interest groups and coalitions of interest groups. In recent years, this dependence on interest group coalitions has become the dominant public policy.[20] Many of the most thoughtful and active proponents of planned change in American society today are vigorous proponents of a coalition strategy, although sometimes for the wrong reasons.

Coalitions are rarely possible, however, without compromise. They may be, and often are, formed initially without any compromise, but seldom can they be sustained without compromises on tactics, strategy, leadership, and even occasionally on issues. The agent of change who believes compromise is a dirty word will not be as effective as the person who is honestly convinced that the suggestions of others may improve the original proposal for change. In addition to improving the quality of the proposal, an openness to compromise often helps members of the supporting group identify with the plans for change and enables them to suggest improvements in strategy and tactics.

This leads into the sixth, and what may be the most essential, element in an effective supporting group. This is the capability of the members of the supporting group to take an idea or a proposal for change that is a response to discontent and that has been developed by the smaller initiating group and to revise or modify it and to adopt it as "ours!" This almost invariably means some compromises between the proposal for change developed by members of the original initiating group and the suggestions emerging from persons or factions that constitute the larger supporting group. The complexity of this is intensified when the time dimension is recognized. This means that as the supporting group grows with the passage of time, and as new persons or groups join this alliance, the proposal for change is being reworked and revised, compromises are being arrived at, and a growing number of individuals and groups feel a personal identification with the proposal for change.

One of the more remarkable dimensions of this process is that as the proposal which originated back in the smaller initiating group is subjected to amendment, revision, compromise, and alteration, it is improved in quality. (That is a very threatening statement for those of us who believe that when we give birth to a proposal for change, it is perfect from the moment it is born and can never be improved.)

For the change agent this means he should not only look at this concept of a supporting group for political reasons, but also as a means of improving the quality of the proposals for change and for developing a process of planned change which is of a continuing nature. This is a sharp contrast to the traditional view of change as a series of isolated and distinct episodes each separate from another in both time and process.

John W. Gardner has spoken of this in his plea for a "self-renewing society." In his 1969 Godkin Lectures at Harvard he said, "Each reformer comes to his task with a little bundle of desired changes. The implication is that if appropriate reforms are carried through and the defects corrected, the society will be wholly satisfactory and the work of the reformer done. That is a primitive way of viewing social change." [21] Gardner goes on to point out the necessity of a continuous process of renewal (change) and the importance of coalitions.

The change-oriented individual may want to ask himself several questions as he reflects on the concept of the supporting group in the process of intentional change. First, is he *primarily* interested in making a public witness to dramatize the issue and to increase the degree of discontent, *or* is he primarily interested in change? If the latter, it is difficult to overstate the crucial importance of this third step in the process of planned change. The partial or total neglect of this phase of the process is unquestionably the largest single cause of failures in efforts at planned change.

Second, is he primarily committed to seeing that *his* ideas for change are adopted *or* in helping to achieve change? If the former, he runs the risk of skipping or minimizing this third phase of the process. If the latter, he will have much less difficulty in building a supporting group and helping it revise and improve any proposals coming out of the initiating group.

Third, is he willing and able to submerge his own role, or is he the type of individual who tends to have a very high degree of visibility as an advocate of change? The vast majority of effective organizers of influential supporting groups tend to be drawn from the ranks of the low-visibility change agents. In an era when there is a very rapidly growing emphasis on the concept of shared or participatory or collaborative leadership, this is a point of increasing importance. With the exception of a few charismatic figures like Walter Reuther and Martin Luther King, Jr., who could fill both roles, the headlines tend to be devoted to the highly visible advocates of change, but the low-visibility enabling types tend to produce the results.

Finally, is he consciously aware of the need to follow through? The process of planned change frequently seems to require "one more effort." The women's rights amendment failed to pass in the Senate in 1970 because that one extra effort to build one more supporting group was missing.

111

## Implementation

In a great many efforts at planned change this fourth phase in the process is a mere formality. If all of the homework has been done in the first three steps, this fourth step of implementation may appear to be both unexciting and easy.

The nature and form of this fourth step varies tremendously. It may be the election of a reform candidate to public office. It may be securing adoption of a constitutional amendment as in the case of the women's rights amendment. It may be the sale of a piece of property, construction of a building, or adoption of a new program. It may be the signing of a truce or a treaty of peace.

It often requires the establishment or creation of a group of individuals who will carry on from this point. The election of a slate of new city council members or the founding of a new congregation or the establishment of a new college or the shifting of responsibility from one department to another (either new or old) are examples of the establishment of an implementation group.

In many of these examples that moment when the proponents of change can say "We won!" marks the dividing line between advocating change and implementing change.

The skills and resources required on one side of this dividing line often vary tremendously from the skills and resources that are most useful on the other. A common example of this is the candidate for public office who appears to have all the assets necessary to be a very effective office seeker, but who turns out to possess few of the talents necessary to be an effective officeholder. The United States

Senate usually has ten to twenty individuals who fit this description in every session.

In most efforts at implementing change four resources are necessary. Frequently these must be mobilized from the general community. The first is a skill in the implementation of ideas. This often is a different skill, and not infrequently a different type of personality, than that necessary for generating new ideas or for organizing support for change. Again the United States Senate supplies many examples. In every presidential election year one or two or three senators are mentioned as potential presidential candidates (because of their effectiveness at getting their proposals implemented into law in the Senate), but rarely is one of these highly skillful senators nominated for the presidency—which is a very different type of leadership position.

A second resource is personnel. In this case the reference is to the persons who are able to turn the power generated by an effort at change into the channels that cause things to happen. In every organization there are the full-time professionals who have the capacity to support and turn into reality a proposal for change—and also the capability to smother most proposals between the time of approval and the point of implementation. A useful truism to remember is that the most enthusiastic and skillful advocate of change, working at this on only a part-time schedule, seldom can prevail over the mediocre full-time professional who is committed to blocking every proposal for change.

Karl Hertz has spoken to the same basic issue in describing some of the protest movements of the 1960s. "The protest movements, despite all their brave talk about indigenous leadership, are not training leaders for the daily routine of urban politics. . . . For it is administration, finally, which converts legislation into social reality, . . . especially in the human services—welfare, urban renewal, war against poverty." [22]

A third essential resource is goodwill. Even the most righteous and relevant efforts at planned social change have little chance of success if they are attempted in an atmosphere filled with distrust, hostility, and enmity. This may be a far more important consideration in the process of intentional change today than ever before.

The fourth resource that is essential to the implementation stage is loyalty. This includes both the continued loyalty of the members of the supporting group and the loyalty of the recently identified allies who may have come into this implementation stage from a different point of entry or for different reasons. To move ahead to an issue discussed at greater length in Chapter 7, the loyalty must be to those introducing the change or to the change itself. If the loyalty is to the organization, to the previous leaders, to the past, to tradition, or to "the old ways of doing things," it becomes a barrier to change. Here again the vital importance of loyalty to the new and to the advocates of change becomes most apparent when it is absent. This generalization applies to the State Department, the United States Senate, the institutional expression of the church, the public school, and the widowed husband who brings home a new mother for his children.

### Freezing the Change

The final step in the process of planned social change is to institutionalize or freeze the new set of conditions. This can be accomplished by a variety of methods. An authoritarian political leader may be elected to his nation's highest office and then declare himself in office for life. It is possible to take certain irreversible steps and thus freeze the new change. It would be very difficult today to repeal the Social Security Act, which had so much opposition when it was passed in 1935 that the Congress adjourned without appropriating the funds necessary to implement it, or to repeal the constitutional amendments abolishing slavery or giving women the right to vote or granting to the Federal Government the power to levy an income tax.

In looking at these and other changes which have been institutionalized, it is helpful to turn again to Kurt Lewin's concept of an equilibrium resulting from the pressure of opposing forces. Once change has been secured, what must be done to the restraining forces on one side of the move toward change or to the driving forces on the side to stablize the equilibrium at the new point?

It took a remarkably powerful Secretary of Defense, Robert S. McNamara, to reallocate the power of decision-making on the choice of weapons in the Pentagon from the military leaders to the civilian specialists. With his departure, part of the driving force that had accomplished this change disappeared, and it was not possible to maintain the equilibrium at the new point.

Another approach to institutionalizing change can be seen in the legislative process by which a new program is approved with a very modest appropriation being required, but with built-in requirements for a much higher level of expenditures in subsequent years. Veterans' benefits, the

1968 Housing Act, the Model Cities program, Medicare, Social Security, and federal aid to education are examples of this approach to institutionalizing change.

In looking at the basic issue of institutionalizing change at the new equilibrium, the agent of change may find it helpful to ask himself three questions.

First, is it necessary, or even desirable, to freeze or to make permanent this new set of conditions? Frequently the answer will be in the negative. It may be necessary to go through all of the first four steps in the process to get the local Chamber of Commerce to jointly sponsor the Fourth of July fireworks program with the local Federation of Labor, but it may not be desirable to make this a permanent arrangement. It may take considerable time and effort to persuade the local Board of Education to permit the high school seniors to participate in a tutorial program for disadvantaged children, but it may not be desirable to make this a permanent part of board policy.

In general, if a change in traditions or customs is sought for one event, it is unnecessary and may even be unwise to institutionalize that change. On the other hand, if a basic change in policy is sought, as contrasted to an exception to the policy, it often is necessary to freeze the new set of conditions. Frequently this takes time, energy, skill, and money. An outstanding example is the Legal Defense Fund of the NAACP which has been called on in hundreds of cases to maintain a change at the new point of equilibrium.

The second question is a more complex one than the first. How can the advocates of change freeze the changed set of circumstances? While the answer to that question varies with the circumstances, the same four points keep reappearing. (1) Increasingly, legislation, the law, and the courts are involved in institutionalizing change. (2) The resources (skill, personnel, goodwill, and loyalty) necessary for implementation tend to be the same resources required for freezing the change. (3) Persistence is the name of the game throughout the process of planned change, from enlarging the degree of discontent to freezing the new point of equilibrium. (4) The larger or the more firmly bound up in tradition the organization, the more difficult it is to institutionalize a change unless the values, direction, and orientation of the organization are changed. (See Chapter 7 for an elaboration of this point.)

The third question is the one the agent of change will find most difficult to answer. How can the change be stabilized at this point of equilibrium to prevent a slipping back to the former state of affairs, but not fixed so rigidly that the current effort at freezing will be a barrier to further change in the future?

There is no easy answer to this question, but the importance of the basic issue can be illustrated by looking at the current status of the trade union movement, or the welfare system, or free public education, or the congregational polity of the churches (at this point the denominational label on the congregation has little relevance if it pays all its bills), or the requirement of a seminary degree for ordination, or the exemption of church-owned real estate from taxation, or the right of every municipality to adopt its own set of land use controls (a right that was institutionalized by the United States Supreme Court in 1926 and a right that will be sharply curtailed by the United States Supreme Court during the next dozen years).[23]

In addition to analyzing the process of planned social change, it may be helpful for the agent of change to look at another dimension of this subject. If ignored, it can become a serious barrier to change.

## The Counterstrategy

Except in the event of a crisis, every effort at internally motivated change is met with resistance. Every theory of how to achieve change produces a theory of how to counter the first theory. There often is a lag between the emergence of the resistance and the formulation of an anti-change strategy, but the agent of change can count on its emergence.

An outstanding recent example of the formalized emergence of a counterstrategy has been in the field of higher education. In 1967 and 1968 many university administrators were caught unprepared, and their responses to confrontation tactics often left them at a serious disadvantage in subsequent negotiations. By early 1969 a series of guidelines for a counterstrategy had begun to be developed. These included a preference for the use of the courts and injunctions to clear buildings that had been occupied by students rather than calling in the police, a preference to keep the university open if at all possible, creating acceptable channels for dissent and protest, the direct involvement of students and faculty with the administration in making policy decisions in response to student protest (this sharing of authority produced a sharing of responsibility almost immediately in direct proportion to the degree to which authority actually was shared), and a general rejection of the concept of amnesty.

By late 1970 the President's Commission on Campus Unrest had formalized a counterstrategy which included defining in advance the limits of permissible conduct, an emphasis on negotiation rather than confrontation, the waiting out of a nonviolent incident to see if it dissipates on its own, the use of court injunctions (which changes the lineup of participants in the struggle; when an injunction is issued the conflict becomes one of the protester versus the courts rather than the protester versus the university), and the use of disciplinary and judicial procedures.[24]

The development of a counterstrategy can be seen in other efforts at change ranging from the granting of public funds for private schools to legalizing abortion to changing the dress code in high school to granting the clientele a voice in policy-making in the institutions and structures that dominate their lives to a revision of the tax structure. The counterstrategy used by opponents of television documentaries, which apparently find their mark, has been described in interesting detail by a former colleague of the late Edward Murrow.[25]

Perhaps the two common threads that run through an analysis of efforts at change and the attempts to formulate a counterstrategy are: (1) Sooner or later one or both parties probably will turn to the legal system of the organization or to the courts. (2) The counterstrategy will include an attack on the motivation, reliability, or credentials of the advocates of change. Translated into everyday language, this means that in formulating his initial strategy and in planning to respond to a counterstrategy the agent of change should be prepared for an attack on both personal and legal grounds. Among other implications this means he should examine the legal basis of his position and determine how the ground rules of the organization or the laws of the state can be exploited by both opponents and proponents of the effort at change.[26]

All of these considerations in the process of planned social change presuppose a style of leadership by the agent of change that includes both an interest and a skill in anticipating the future. While this is not always a safe presumption, increasingly the advocate of change must move toward an anticipatory style of leadership if he is to be effective. This is one of the characteristics that stands out in a review of the role and style of the contemporary change agent in American society.[27]

# 4

# Questions for the Change Agent

In December, 1967, Allard Lowenstein convened the Conference of Concerned Democrats in Chicago as a part of the movement to replace President Lyndon B. Johnson as the nominee of the Democratic Party in 1968. The persons invited were the kind who "wouldn't frighten the suburban housewife," and it was obvious that this meeting was called for action rather than show.

One person who also had attended the New Politics Conference earlier that fall spoke of the contrast and described Lowenstein's meeting as "much duller, but more effective."

This incident illustrates one of the seven basic questions confronting every advocate of intentional change. This first question can be phrased in these words, "Should I work for change from within the organization, attempting to build alliances with other persons who can facilitate change? Or should I concentrate my efforts on a dramatic and highly visible effort to arouse people to the nature of the problem in the hope that once they see the urgency of the problem, their discontent will cause them to join me in working for change?"

There is no universal answer that will fit every person and every situation. More often than not the personality of the individual, rather than the situation, will be the controlling force in making the choice between these two alternatives. At the Chicago meeting it was clear that Allard Lowenstein was attempting to work as an insider and to win allies from among the discontented members of the Democratic Party.

Not infrequently, the advocate of change will begin by attempting to call attention to the problem, to raise the level of discontent, and to function as a highly visible "prophetic witness" type of change agent. Subsequently, when the level of discontent has been raised and potential allies are beginning to appear, this same individual will shift to the alternative approach and begin to build a coalition around the original initiating group.

This raises the second basic question for the advocate of intentional change. When is the appropriate time to switch tactics from arousing discontent to building a coalition? Again there is no simple answer, and this may be the question which suggests that being an effective change agent is as much an art as a skill. While he occasionally obscures this point with a flood of picturesque rhetoric, Saul Alinsky has repeatedly contended that the timing in this change of tactics is one of the marks of an effective organizer and change agent.

This point can be illustrated by again turning to the selection of a Democratic nominee for the presidency in 1968. One of the reasons for Lowenstein's effectiveness in "encouraging" President Johnson not to run in 1968 was the timing in his change of tactics from a public display of discontent to building alliances. Likewise one of the reasons for Senator Eugene McCarthy's diminishing support in 1968 was his inability or his unwillingness to change from a highly visible symbol of discontent with the status quo to an active agent of change who could help build a broad-based supporting coalition for change.

This raises a third question for the advocate of planned change, a question concerning style or role.

### Three Styles

"Well, I was pretty certain I would see you here today," said a gray-haired university professor to a thirty-five-year-old minister as they shivered in the chill autumn wind while waiting for the peace march to begin.

"You shouldn't have had any doubts," replied the clergyman with a smile. "This is a part of my calling. We have to turn this country around and the best way to do that is to dramatize the issues and focus public attention on the problems."

"No one can accuse you of neglecting your responsibility to witness to your convictions," responded the professor. "You've marched in Selma with the welfare rights mothers and for peace. You've picketed the manufacturers of napalm and the White House, and here at home you've helped block the eastside freeway. The people in your congregation certainly should know where you stand on the issues of the day!"

"You turned down a $12,000-a-year beginning salary with the largest law firm in the state to go with a storefront OEO legal-aid office for $600 a month?"·asked an incredulous father of his twenty-four-year-old daughter who had just graduated from law school with honors.

"I had no choice," replied his daughter. "We have to turn this country around and the law is the best way to do it. Look at what has been done already. OEO lawyers have been able to get the residency requirement for welfare recipients thrown out. They have helped make divorce available to the poor as well as the rich. They have blocked the use of braceros in California, and they have changed the whole national attitude toward public assistance. They really know how to get things done!"

"You're too old for the Peace Corps! They don't want old men like you, Hank, they're looking for college graduates in their twenties," explained Charlie Brandt to his forty-six-year-old brother, Henry. The two brothers had farmed together for a quarter of a century and were in the process of selling their 1,300-acre farm to Charlie's two married sons. Charlie already had a job lined up with the county highway department, but the younger brother, Henry, had been very secretive about his plans until this family picnic when he suddenly announced that he and his wife, Mildred, had been accepted by the Peace Corps.

"As usual, you're about six years behind times," replied Henry. "Today the Peace Corps is looking for mature persons with skills that are needed in some of the underdeveloped countries. One of the biggest needs is for farmers. The gap between the haves and the have-nots is widening rapidly and unless we can change that trend, the whole world is headed for disaster. We have to do a lot more to help people help themselves. As far as Mildred and I can see, the only way we can make the changes that have to be made in this old world is to enable people to help themselves. That's what the Peace Corps is all about and that's why your kid brother is starting a new career."

These three individuals illustrate three of the styles or roles open to the contemporary change agent. Again there is no answer as to which is the "right" style or the "wrong" approach. The clergyman's style was that of the prophetic witness in the Old Testament tradition, who focused public attention on what he identified as the evils of the day.

The youthful law school graduate saw that in terms of her skills and her personality the logical style was to work as an active change agent from outside the system, but using the procedures and methods on which the system has been built.

The forty-six-year-old farmer saw that in terms of his personality and his skills the community development approach of the Peace Corps was the appropriate style for him.[1]

There is another dimension to this question of the style of the advocate of change that does have a more direct answer. This is the question of leadership style.

## The Death of Big Daddy

One of the classic images of the effective politician has been the precinct captain, the ward leader, the alderman, or the congressman who devoted a large portion of his time and energy to taking care of his constituents' needs. He found a job for the unemployed son, he delivered Thanksgiving and Christmas baskets to the homes of the poor, he saw that a load of coal was delivered to the widow's house in January when her meager funds could not carry her through the unusually cold winter, he "fixed" your traffic ticket, and he saw to it that a streetlight was moved so it did not shine into your bedroom.

He took care of the problems of his constituents in an effective, but paternalistic, manner that often earned him the label of "Big Daddy." In his own way, Big Daddy could get things done. He was one model of a change agent.

His counterpart could be found in many of the industrial and business leaders of the last third of the nineteenth century and the first four or five decades of this century. Henry Ford was a remarkable example of the Big Daddy leader in business.

His counterpart also could be found among merchants, bankers, landlords, generals, teachers, plantation owners, bishops, husbands, college presidents, morticians, ranchers, pastors, athletic coaches, fathers, union leaders, physicians, and scores of other leaders.

126

The big news of the last half of the twentieth century is that Big Daddy is dead. This may be the biggest news of this era.

A great many people have not yet heard about Big Daddy's death, others have heard but do not believe it, and there is also a large number who have heard and who know Big Daddy is gone, but have not yet been able to adjust their own style of leadership to the new realities.

Big Daddy's death was the result of a complex assortment of factors. The list includes the democratic spirit which has toppled many other great American traditions, free public education, the Western frontier, the tremendous increase in the economic resources of the nation, the black revolution, the Christian ethic, research by behavioral scientists, mobility, enlargement of the right to vote, labor unions, the youth revolt of the late 1960s, the independence of the judiciary, and many other forces.

One of the first public announcements of Big Daddy's death came in 1960 with publication of *The Human Side of Enterprise,* by Douglas McGregor.[2] In this he formalized his proposal that the conventional approach to leadership and management was based on a series of propositions that presupposed people were passive, perhaps even lazy, and had to be motivated by a system of rewards and punishments.[3] This he called "Theory X."

McGregor proposed that a more appropriate approach to leadership and management should be based on what he called "Theory Y." This presumes that "people can achieve their own goals *best* by directing *their own* efforts toward organizational objectives." [4]

Another announcement of Big Daddy's death was made by Gerald J. Jud a few years later.[5] He pointed out that in both the local church and the denominational agencies "the Big Daddy syndrome" and "the Trickle Down Theory of church leadership" are obsolete forms of leadership style. In this extraordinarily well-written and provocative essay, Jud called for a new style of collaborative leadership.

More recently *Harper's* magazine carried a pair of articles under the headlined title of "Whatever. Happened to the 'Big Daddies'?"[6] The first article discussed the decline and fall of Adam Clayton Powell, "Prince of Harlem," and the second reviewed the changing career of Jess Unruh, "a former kingmaker," from California.

The trend is largely, but not completely, away from the Big Daddy style and in the direction of a participatory style of leadership for the effective agent of change. Collaboration, not coercion, is the style appropriate for most points of planned social change in both public and private organizations and institutions in the last third of this century.[7]

This raises the fourth in this series of basic questions for the advocate of planned change.

Does he know Big Daddy is dead?

## How Do You Get Things Done?

A frequently neglected responsibility that is a part of the new style of leadership concerns the strategy and tactics for implementing proposals for change.

As Roger Shinn has pointed out, "Society usually moves only under the impulse of aggressive leadership which is in some sense elite."[8] But this does not mean it has to be the

Big Daddy style. One element of effective collaborative leadership, which may be perceived by some as elitist or even as dictatorial, is the possession and application of a general frame of reference or system for bringing about change.

Education, moral persuasion, and legal procedures have been three of the traditional means of bringing about social change. All three have been under serious attack recently because they do not produce (1) instant results or (2) the esprit de corps that often is produced by the direct action approach.

Another approach to this issue is to look at the "4 Cs" which describe four contrasting methods:

1. Coercion

   This is the application of authority and power and the necessary degree of force to produce the desired results. Adoption of this approach encourages an emphasis on power and the acquisition of power.

2. Co-optation

   This emphasizes bringing the opposition into the supporting group. From one side it is described as being open to diverse points of views. From the other side it is sometimes described as "buying off the opposition."

3. Conflict

   This means the battle lines must be drawn and the potential conflict turned into a reality before any resolution can be achieved. Frequently conflict helps to clarify the issues, but the price tag often is delay.

4. Cooperation
This is the most widely used approach in both public and private affairs. The obvious limitation is that it often is useful in only the second or third stage when major changes are contemplated. A related limitation is that, like the use of conflict, it usually is very time-consuming.

Each of these alternatives also has limitations or disadvantages. There is no perfect method or approach with many advantages and no disadvantages. Each method has a price tag on it.

A third approach to change is built on the presumption that there exist unitary power structures, or at least a series of power centers. The community-action concept popularized in the war on poverty during the last decade was based on this presumption. But this again does not provide a clear understanding of what is to happen. To the followers of Saul Alinsky, community action meant a confrontation with the power structure. To those who worked in the Gray Areas programs of the Ford Foundation, community action meant organizing the power centers for a more effective response to the problems of the inner city. To others, it meant expanding the power structure in order to deal with the problems of juvenile delinquency, while to the Department of Agriculture, it has meant collaboration with the power structure. In each case the community-action approach to change also has had a price tag on it.

Unless this point is recognized, unless the advocates of change recognize that every approach to planned social change has built-in deficiencies, limitations, and incompatibilities, the change agent is likely to fall into the trap described by Daniel Patrick Moynihan: "We constantly underestimate difficulties, overpromise results, and avoid any evidence of incompatibility and conflict, thus repeatedly creating the conditions of failure out of a desperate desire for success." [9]

This raises the fifth question for the change agent. "What is your approach to getting things done and what is the price tag on that approach?"

## What Are the Rules?

One of the most important recent reversals of policy in the House of Representatives occurred in March, 1971, when to the great surprise of most observers, the House voted 217 to 204 to cut off funds for the supersonic transport plane (SST). This reversed a pattern of seven years of consistent support for the SST by the House.

The key change agent in this episode was Illinois Congressman Sidney Yates. He offered an amendment to delete funds for the SST from an appropriation for the Department of Transportation. Just before the vote he said, "Mr. Chairman, I demand tellers with clerk."

This meant that members of the House had to cast a roll-call vote for or against the amendment or be counted absent.

This was the first occasion that a new rule was used in the House.[10] Until 1971 it was not possible for a member to require a public record of how each member voted on a proposed amendment to legislation. The "reform package" adopted to be effective in January, 1971, meant that it no longer was possible for a member to hide behind an anonymous teller vote or to be absent and thus hide from public opinion. When Yates asked for "tellers with clerk," it meant that every member's position on the SST would be public knowledge. The result was first of all a remarkably large vote. Second, it meant that many who did not want to cut off funds, but who could not take such a position publicly, had to vote against the SST. They could not afford the political consequences of voting against the amendment or of not voting. Third, it demonstrated again that one of the most valuable resources of a change agent is to know the rules of the game.

The rules will vary from one situation to another. They may be expressed in one or more of several forms. This may include the articles of incorporation, the by-laws, the precedents, *Robert's Rules of Order,* custom, judicial rulings, zoning, the laws of the church, the budget, seniority, or deed restrictions on the use of land. Occasionally, as in the House of Representatives, the rules are stated very formally; more often they have never been completely codified.

But wherever he is, and regardless of the circumstances, sooner or later the agent of change will find himself confronted with the question, "What are the rules here?"

## Hard Choices and Simplistic Solutions

One of the biggest pitfalls before the advocate of change is the attractiveness of simplistic solutions to complex problems. The recent history of planned change is filled with examples.

In the 1950s it was believed low-rent, publicly owned, and subsidized housing was a large part of the answer for the problems facing low-income families. By 1950 the nation had over a dozen years of experience with more than a score of public housing projects across the country. This "solution" was widely accepted by liberal advocates of change in Washington and in dozens of cities. Large public housing projects, accommodating hundreds of low-income families, were constructed in New York, Cleveland, Chicago, St. Louis, and other cities. One result was that they greatly intensified the problems of the families living there for a sustained period of time. Fifteen years after it was completed, the St. Louis Housing Authority proposed complete demolition of the $36-million, 33-building Pruitt Igoe project. The 2,800-unit development had never been fully occupied and had come to be regarded as a jungle.[11]

A popular dogma among urban renewal planners twenty years ago was that hospitals and institutions of higher education were excellent anchor points for developing a redevelopment plan for a community or neighborhood. Scores of urban renewal plans were prepared which included hospital, college, or university as one of the major land users. Typically, these plans provided for the expansion of the hospital or university, for new housing, for an improved traffic pattern, and for other changes necessary to make a "better" neighborhood. In 1959 the Congress canonized this concept with passage of Section 112 as an amendment to the National Housing Act.

By the early 1960s it had become apparent to many residents of these communities and to some planners that the hospitals and institutions of higher education were not allies in the process of building a better community; they were enemies. The presumed alliance was based on the common characteristic that, like the residents, these institutions were land users; but it became apparent that another far more critical characteristic separated them. Until relatively recently the basic, and often the only, orientation of these institutions was to the clientele, not to the neighborhood. Since few of the clients came from the immediate neighborhood, the priorities of these institutions rarely coincided with the priorities of the residents. How should that piece of land at the corner be used? As a playground for children from the neighborhood? As a parking lot for visitors to the hospital? As a site for housing for student nurses? As a site for low-rent housing for elderly residents of the neighborhood?

Many other examples of simple solutions to complex problems can be offered. In 1965 it was a popular belief among many white churchmen that one part of the solution to the race problem was a racially inclusive church and that the racial integration of previously all-white congregations should be vigorously encouraged. By 1967 the message from black churchmen was beginning to be heard. This is one of the most effective means of killing off the strongest institution in the Negro community.

In the 1956 to 1962 era one of the most widely advocated answers to the problems of urban America was metropolitan government. By 1963 it was apparent that this also was a means of diluting the political power of blacks, of encouraging the taxpayer rebellion, of increasing racial tensions, and of heightening the sense of depersonalization and the degree of alienation among metropolitan residents.[12]

During the past several years the housing shortage, especially for low- and low-middle-income families, has become an increasingly acute problem. A major emphasis in the response to this problem by white liberal advocates of change has been to "open up the suburbs" to the poor, the black, and the elderly by increasing the quantity of subsidized housing.

While this approach has much to be commended on ideological and humanitarian grounds, there is considerable evidence to suggest that if the problem is a shortage of housing and a limited range of housing choices open to people in the lower half of the economic ladder, the major emphasis should be on the construction of homes costing over $30,000 or apartments renting for more than $300 a month. While this will sound offensive to many, the fact remains that construction of one $30,000 home enables, on the average, four families to move as contrasted to the construction of one $15,000 home which enables, again on the average, only two families to move.[13]

In the 1935 to 1970 era this nation undertook, encouraged, and carried through a radical approach to the "farm problem." This is sometimes referred to as "the technological revolution in agriculture." In 1935, 20 percent of the labor force was required to provide the food for 127 million people. In 1970, 4 percent of the labor force was able to feed a population that had passed the 200-million mark. Dr. Robert Steadman, staff director of the Committee for Economic Development, has called this technological revolution a "social disaster" and pointed to the revolutionary changes in agriculture as the source of many of the social, economic, and family problems facing the nation today. He pointed to the family farm with its concept of the extended family as a means of providing additional protection, security, and care for the young, the aged, and the single adults; American society has not been able to provide a satisfactory substitute for this since the sudden disappearance of the family farm.[14]

At this point the reader asks, "Well, if everything he does turns out to cause more harm than good, what should the advocate of change do?"

This again is a very complex question and illustrates the point: Often there are no easy or simple answers. One approach is for the advocate of change to build his problem-solving approach on a broader philosophical base or on a set of operating principles which will help him respond in those situations where there is no single "best" answer.

## The Change Agent's Baggage

Every individual brings with him his own perspective, his own set of past experiences, his own set of values, and his own set of biases, prejudices, and assumptions. Whether these can be dignified with the term "a philosophy" is debatable, but not very important. What is extremely important is that the advocate of change, whether he is working from the inside as a member of the organization or from the outside as a change agent or a consultant, be aware of the baggage he carries with him and of the implications of this load.

What are the items a change agent might carry in his baggage? Here are a few suggestions:

1. An outsider cannot solve an organization's problems,

but frequently he can help increase the organization's capability to solve its own problems.

2. Every problem has more than one possible solution.

3. The cost-benefit theory is always at work. Every goal and every change from the status quo has a price tag on it.

4. The consultant should have a generalization behind every specific comment, suggestion, or recommendation, and a particular or specific point to illustrate every generalization.

5. One of the most significant pieces of baggage carried by every advocate of change is his previous experience in similar situations. If used as a guide, this may be a great asset. If viewed as offering the same answer to every problem, it can be a major liability.

6. The easiest, the most tempting, and the least creative response to conflict within an organization is to pretend it does not exist.

7. As an organization becomes more sensitive to the needs of people, its operation increases in complexity and the intuitive response tends to be counterproductive.

8. Every organization is governed by a series of unwritten policy statements, usually referred to as customs, traditions, or "this is the way we have always done it." Often a part of the change agent's task is to help the client identify, evaluate, and revise these unwritten policy statements.

9. The most powerful factor in the decision-making in an organization is precedent. The older or the larger the organization, the more powerful is precedent.

10. The institutional or organizational framework in which an individual functions limits the degree of change

that can be accomplished by changes in the individual. This ceiling can be raised only by changes in the values, attitudes, orientation, traditions, and customs of the organization and of the people in it. (See Chapter 7.)

11. Every organization, but especially nonprofit organizations which do not have easy-to-read evaluations of the fulfillment of purpose, tend to move survival and institutional maintenance to the top of the priority list.

12. Every outside consultant and many inside advocates of change have a "contract" with the client. This contract includes the expectations of the client. Often the expectations of the client change during the process of the consultation. The advocate of change should be sensitive to these changing expectations.

13. Education is alienating, and every effort by the advocate of change to educate or train individuals in an organization will tend to alienate those individuals from other persons in the organization.

14. "Unless you know where you're going, any road will take you there." [15]

15. "Humor is a social lubricant that helps us get over some of the bad spots. . . . Humor is a humanizing agent." [16]

This raises the last in this series of questions for the change agent, "What do you carry around with you in your baggage?"

**5**

# The Use of Power and Social Change

One of the better-known Protestant church magazines recently carried two related editorials. In the first it strongly supported the concept of "Power to the People!" The editor declared that only by recognizing the validity of this ideal could the churches participate meaningfully in the contemporary American revolution.

A few months later, an editorial was devoted to a proposal for restructuring the denominational organization. In commenting on this, the same editor gave restrained support to a plan calling for the decentralization of power in the denomination, and added that power must be placed close enough to the people that they can be heard, but far enough away that the people cannot determine policy on social and political issues by majority vote.

This episode illustrates the dilemma faced by the founding fathers as they sought to draft a constitution for a new nation. This classic dilemma can be seen very clearly in the political philosophy of James Madison and in his inability to reconcile these two conflicting goals.[1]

This episode also illustrates a major dilemma facing the agent of change who is concerned with the use of power in the process and dynamics of planned social change. On the one hand, it is tempting to support the ideal of maximizing the degree of power in the hands of each individual. On the other hand, there comes the stark realization that power can be used, not only to accomplish change, but also to still the prophetic voice, to thwart proposals for change, and to perpetuate the status quo. Hence the pragmatic desire to inhibit the power of the majority often conflicts with a strong democratic bias in any discussion of the location or the exercise of power.

This suggests that an examination of the use of power in the process of intentional social change requires an understanding of the nature of power, the exercise of power, the sources of power, the location or place of power, and the contemporary redistribution of power, as well as of the ethical considerations that influence the use of power. These factors are as important to the change process as the political philosophy of the change agent, whether he is a republican elitist or a democratic populist.

## The Nature of Power

What is power? This question can be answered from several perspectives. One of the most helpful is to look at the nature of power.

In a pioneering essay, published nearly two decades ago, Herbert Simon described power in interpersonal terms, or the capability of causing a change in behavior.[2] This was a very important contribution, since it broadened the traditional definition of power as primarily a means of influencing decision-making. The more limited definition had been popularized by a series of writers from Thomas Hobbes to Bertrand Russell to Harold Lasswell. Simon's broadened definition of the nature of power makes it easier to see both the overt and the covert uses of power. It also includes the frequent exercise of power in preventing decisions from being made as well as the use of power in making decisions.

Simon's concept of the nature of power is of special interest to the proponent of planned change who finds himself seeking to change the behavior of both individuals and organizations. The broader definition of Simon's has become the operational definition of power for many individuals seeking to change either the secular or the ecclesiastical structures of society. It also is often the working definition of the person who comes to a position that was thought to be filled with power, but finds himself unable to change the direction of the organization or of the people in it. This frustration often is shared by a newly elected president of the United States, by a new congressman, by a new Negro mayor, by a new denominational executive, by a new superintendent of schools, or by a new minister in a local church. This reflects one aspect of the nature of power. Power often appears to be greater in the eye of the beholder than it is in the hands of the holder. A well-known community organizer has suggested this canard should be turned around and exploited by the community. He contends that the organizer's enemy usually overestimates the power of the organizer, and therefore one of Alinsky's thirteen basic rules of power tactics is to take advantage of this.[3]

Two other very useful insights into the nature of power have been contributed by A. A. Berle. Berle insists that power "invariably fills any vacuum in human organization" and always prevails over chaos.[4] Whether the vacuum is caused by a political leader who fails to exercise the full authority of his office or the electric traffic signal that malfunctions or the strike of a municipal police force, the vacuum is filled by forces for order. Any chaotic conditions that result from the sudden vacuum are always temporary as a new source of power fills the vacuum.

This aspect of the nature of power appears to be neglected by one group of contemporary radical revolutionaries who see anarchy as the best road to social change. It also appears to be behind the warnings of those who are concerned that an increase in civil disorder bordering on chaos may produce a very repressive political regime.

A second highly relevant contribution by Berle is that a precondition of *lasting* power is the combination of an idea, system, or philosophy and an institutional structure for the utilization of power.[5] These two elements are an integral part of the power held by a street gang in Chicago, the city government of Atlanta, the Democratic Party, the Southern Baptist Convention, or the minister of a local church. This has a very high degree of relevance for the change agent who is convinced he can continue to function effectively on the basis of charisma and derides those who want to develop a philosophical base or build an organizational structure.

Another characteristic of the nature of power deserves serious consideration by the individual interested in planned social change. *The exercise of power is determined by values and relationships.* While it is true that the possession of power can be identified by the ability to affect the behavior of others, it also is true that this is rarely a permanent condition. Coercion or the capacity to coerce is dependent upon values and relationships. The power to coerce cannot exist except in relational terms. Parents usually have more power to affect the behavior of a four-year-old than has a person outside the family circle; but twenty years later, as a result of changing relationships and new values, many persons outside the family circle may have more power over that twenty-four-year-old than is held by either parent.

The importance, and the limitations on the change process, of values and relationships can be seen most clearly in the many futile efforts to change an organization by replacing a few key leaders or by specialized training for one or two members of the organization. Despite such efforts, unless the values, orientation, direction of the organization, and the relationships of the new leaders to the total organization are changed, the power of the new leaders will be severely circumscribed. (See Chapter 7 for an elaboration of this point.)

Another aspect of this can be seen as the professional agent of change usually finds himself with varying quantities of power in different stages of his career. One of the most difficult problems encountered by a change agent is to have a *current* estimate of his own power and that of his organization. Relationships and values change so rapidly that a month-old appraisal of the power of a community organization can be disastrously misleading. The same sharp and sudden fluctuations can be seen in the power of a partisan political leader or political organization, but they tend to be less frequent than in the life of a community organization or the professional change agent.

While this is not intended to be an exhaustive analysis of the nature of power, it would be premature to leave the subject without mentioning two of the paradoxes of power that tend to be overlooked by proponents of planned change.

The first of these is that at the same time power is being dispersed and shared by a larger number of persons, the power of those in the top leadership positions may be increasing. The president of a college with 3,000 students in 1940 probably had less power than his successor of 1965 who presided over what had become a state university with 15,000 students and a more diffused power structure in which the power was shared among a comparatively large number of individuals.

This tendency for power at the top to increase at the same time power is being gained by an increasing number of people throughout the system is a paradox that often is overlooked by change agents. A widely circulated myth in church circles in the 1960s was that power was quantitatively constant and no one could gain power unless someone else experienced a loss of power. This paradox denies the validity of the myth. One of the most common examples of the application of this paradox is illustrated by the enlarging of the number of committee members from six to sixty. This often is done under the slogan of sharing the power with more people, but frequently the most important result is to greatly increase the power of the chairman.

A second, related paradox is that in contemporary American society a response to the demand for sharing the power may be self-defeating. To use the previous illustration, each of the fifty-four additional members of the committee do attain a degree of increased power. Frequently, however, they are not able to replace the chairman. His power increases; the fifty-four have gained power individually, but they may have been co-opted from the cause or issue or emerging pressure bloc they represented. They have acquired the appearance, perhaps even the position, of power, but they do not have the tools of power, and they are vulnerable to the risk of becoming more concerned with maintaining the institution of which they now are a part than with intentional change.

## The Exercise of Power

The dilemma produced by this paradox illustrates the difference between the apparent possession of power and the capability of exercising power. This distinction often is overlooked by those who use the reputational model for describing the distribution of power. This distinction also is illustrated by the response of the man who was confronted with the statement that he had tremendous power in his community. "Yes, I guess I do," he replied, "as long as I don't try to use it."

The central point here is that too much emphasis often is given to the alleged *possession* of power and too little to the ability to *exercise* power. In looking at the exercise of power the first point to be recognized is the basic relational attribute of power. As was mentioned earlier, power exists only in relationships; it can never be exercised in a vacuum, and its existence depends upon the values and attitudes of the recipient in the relationship. During the past two decades the power of white persons over black people has decreased sharply as a result of the changes in the relationships and values, changes that were almost completely unilateral in their origins.

During the past decade high school principals, military officers, policemen, parents, clergymen, factory owners, and union officials have been discovering that exercise of power is heavily dependent upon relationships and values.

A second basic consideration in any examination of the exercise of power is that power may be exercised in several ways. Bachrach and Baratz use the concept of "the two faces of power" to point out that power is exercised in the decision-making process, but it also is exercised in what they refer to as "nondecision-making." [6] This is a subtle but very important distinction. It is similar to John C. Bennett's distinction between the overt use of power and the covert use of power. [7]

Regardless of the terminology one prefers, the important point is that power frequently is exercised by inaction, by keeping issues from reaching the decision-making point, and by neutralizing potential conflicts. This expression of power tends to have a very low degree of visibility, and only recently has it begun to receive the attention it deserves from those interested in intentional change.

Bachrach and Baratz also offer another significant corrective to much of the contemporary thinking in emphasizing that in many situations power is only one of many factors at work in the decision-making process.[8] Compliance may be the result of the exercise of power, but it also may be the result of identical value systems, of powerless persuasion, of parallel self-interests, or of a combination of forces and factors.

Perhaps the most frustrating issue in the exercise of power is the distinction between the power to veto a decision and the much greater degree of power required to implement a decision. It is relatively easy to acquire the power necessary to veto a proposed course of action, but comparatively difficult to put together the coalition that can rally the power necessary to implement a proposed course of action. The filibuster in the United States Senate is a highly visible illustration of this distinction.

Frequently ardent proponents of intentional change are elated to discover they have garnered sufficient power to veto a proposed course of action. They believe it is but a short and simple step from that point to winning acceptance of their alternative plan, but then they are disillusioned and frustrated at their inability to exercise the degree of power necessary for positive action.

This inability to gain approval for a specific counterproposal often leads to the question, "If we don't have the necessary power, who does hold the power here?"

## Who Has the Power?

During the past two decades three distinctive approaches have emerged in response to the desire to discover who holds the power in a community.

147

The first and most widely publicized has been the reputational method used by Floyd Hunter and other sociologically oriented researchers.[9] They have sought to identify the persons who are reputed to be the power figures in a community. The methodology used tends to produce a picture of a single power pyramid with a power elite at the top of the pyramid.

The second approach is best illustrated by political scientist Robert A. Dahl and his associates, who popularized the notion of a pluralistic power structure composed of many separate power centers.[10]

More recently there has begun to emerge what can be identified as a third approach. Hunter and his followers sought to identify power holders by asking knowledgeable individuals whom they perceived as the key figures in the power structure. Dahl and his fellow political scientists examined key decisions that were made with the expectation that they could identify the holders of power by discovering who influenced the decision-making process. This method usually led to the conclusion that the power in a community was dispersed among a series of power centers with varying degrees of overlapping membership.

The third approach to this question is based on the assumption that the world is much more complicated and the location of power is a far more complex subject than either Hunter or Dahl reported. As could be predicted, this approach has disclosed a very complex distribution of power. Some holders of power can be identified by reputation or by their visible influence in decision-making. Others can be found by looking at "nondecisions," by identifying those who keep things from happening, who prevent issues from being aired, and who prevent potential conflict from becoming actual conflict. In addition, however, closer scrutiny reveals that many events and decisions "just happen." They are not the result of the conscious exercise of power. An understanding of this third approach to the location of power is essential for a meaningful discussion of the origins of World War II or of the pervasive nature of white racism or of the selection of many candidates for public office or why the environment continues to be polluted.

It usually is difficult for active and impatient proponents of social change to acknowledge any degree of validity or relevance in this third approach.

### The Sources of Power

During the 1930s many people shared the belief that wealth was the most important source of power. A decade later force, and especially military force, was widely acclaimed as the primary source of power. More recently organization has been recognized by many as the most significant source of power—first by the proponents of community organizations and more recently by those seeking change through the political processes.

Each one of those views represents part of reality, for each is a source of power. There are many sources of power, however, including not only wealth, force, and organization, but also charisma, convictions, loyalties, the accident of birth, conflict, an understanding of people, and love.

There are many, including Robert M. MacIver, who contend that knowledge is the prime source of power in contemporary American society, and that it is rapidly outdistancing all others in importance.[11] In recent years active proponents of intentional change have begun to appreciate the importance of knowledge as a source of power, although sometimes this new appreciation for the importance of knowledge has been gained only after a few disheartening defeats.

## Power in the Local Church

A relatively simple illustration of the complexity of this subject of power is the local church. Who holds the power in the congregation? What is the source of that power? What are the limitations?

In most congregations there are many persons holding power in the life of that organization. These include not only the minister and the elected leaders, but also others who do not appear to be power figures, but who in fact do have tremendous collective power. If three fourths of the membership strongly disapprove a course of action that has been taken by the official leadership, they may apply sanctions in an effort to reverse that decision and to change the behavior pattern of the leadership. These sanctions may include staying away from (boycotting) the worship services, withholding financial contributions, or transferring their membership to another congregation. These actions constitute the exercise of power.

The leadership may respond with a power play—by tripling their own financial contributions or by recruiting new members. This represents a deliberate change in relationships and values which has the effect of at least partially nullifying the power of the sanctions.

There are a variety of sources of power within a congregation. These include not only the capacity to apply sanctions but also family name, age, tenure in office, charisma, organizational ability, ordination, wealth, a commitment to the central values of the organization, the ability to grant rewards, and control over information. A common example of the last source is the layman who controls the flow of information to the new minister about the congregation, local traditions, finances, and vital interpersonal relationships. By doing this, he is able to maintain a degree of control (power) over the actions of the new minister.

This brief illustration is inserted here for the benefit of those who believe any discussion of power is not germane to the life and operation of the local church or other smaller organizations where decisions appear to be made on a highly personalized basis by informal means.

### The Power of Power

In most discussions of social change, power is viewed as a means of achieving change. During the past decade many church leaders have come to an acceptance of this fact with great reluctance. Power usually is essential for meaningful participation in the community decision-making process— although not for meaningful participation in all forms of decision-making in life.

The rapidly growing interest by the churches in community organization during the past dozen years has been characterized by three strands—the quest for power for the powerless, human resource development, and accelerating the pace of social change.

Nearly every evaluation of community organization efforts, however, tends to reveal two digressions from the original purposes of the organizational effort. The first is the natural tendency for institutional maintenance to move to the top of the priority list and replace the original purposes. The second is that frequently the acquisition and possession of power changes from the means to an end (change) to becoming an end in itself. This can be seen in the change-oriented organization that postpones action until it acquires more power, in the group that refuses to act for fear that defeat might result in a loss of power, and in the decision to enter into a proposed coalition, not because of agreement on goals, but rather because of a desire to gain power through being a member of that coalition.

In very simple terms, this reaffirms that one of the distinctive attributes of power is the power to subvert the original goals of the person or organization. This is a point that was made famous by Lord Acton long ago, but still tends to be overlooked by change-oriented persons. Power by itself is neutral; the possession of power, however, tends to produce a conservative or anti-change orientation in both people and organizations. A comparison of the power and change orientation of members of labor unions in the 1930s and the 1970s is but one of many illustrations of this tendency.

## Power and Participatory Democracy

This raises one of the most interesting and also one of the most frequently misunderstood issues of the day. As was pointed out in the opening paragraphs of this chapter, the slogan "Power to the People!" has widespread appeal in American society today. It usually is proclaimed by and associated with individuals who desire to accelerate the pace of social change.

The historical record suggests, however, that in fact this represents a very conservative and anti-change point of view.

Ever since Students for a Democratic Society (SDS) issued the now famous Port Huron Statement in 1962, the phrase "participatory democracy" has had a popular appeal to change-oriented individuals.[12] It is becoming increasingly apparent, however, that rapid social change and participatory politics are not necessarily concepts with coterminous boundaries. This has become apparent to the editor referred to in the opening paragraphs of this chapter. It is illustrated by the thousands of referenda for school-bond issues and school-tax levies that have been rejected by the voters (remember, knowledge is a major source of power). It can be seen in the scores of successful efforts by broad-based citizen groups to block the completion of a freeway, the construction of a new college, the implementation of an urban renewal project, the retention of a change-oriented teacher in the local high school, the merger of local school districts, the construction of low-rent housing in white suburban communities, or in the rejection by the voters in nine of fourteen states in November, 1970, of proposals to lower the voting age to eighteen.

A study of open housing referenda suggests that the populists (participatory democrats) are less liberal than the elitists (proponents of representative government).[13]

Three of the most unfortunate aspects of the popular contemporary discussion on participatory democracy are: (1) the issues in the delegating of authority, and especially the criteria for authority, have been obscured; (2) like Rousseau, the discussion has neglected the role of factions and parties in the decision-making process; and (3) the tendency to overlook the fact that on nearly all matters or decisions nearly all of the people will in fact be represented indirectly.[14]

This should not be read as an indictment of the concept of participatory democracy. It is simply an effort to point up the centuries-old dilemma referred to earlier. Which is preferable—a broader dispersal of power or an acceleration of the pace of social change? This brings the discussion to what may be the critical issue of the 1970s in any discussion of power and planned social change.

## The Contemporary Dispersal of Power

One of the most widely held beliefs in contemporary American society is that power is increasingly concentrated in the hands of relatively few individuals in the "power structure," or "the establishment," to use a more recent cliché.[15]

From this observer's perspective, that evaluation does not appear to reflect reality. The broad general trend appears to be in the direction of a wider distribution of power, both political and economic, and a general broadening of the societal participation base. The direction of this trend can be seen in the United States Supreme Court decision granting the suffrage to eighteen-year-olds, in the tremendous increase in voter registration among Negroes, and in the recent rapid moves to recognize the legitimacy of "client representation" in policy-making in universities, anti-poverty programs, welfare agencies, the Model Cities program, the public schools, and in choosing delegates to the 1972 Democratic Convention. One of the least noticed but most important of these trends has been the series of court decisions granting "standing" to citizens seeking to bring suit against public agencies and the decisions institutionalizing the "right" of citizen participation in certain community planning ventures.[16] The direction of this trend toward a diffusion of power also can be seen in the family, in the military, in the factories, in the consumer movement, in government, and in the churches.

Despite these signs, both the rightists and the leftists assume that more and more power is being concentrated in fewer and fewer hands. Their assumption is reinforced by the conventional wisdom that an inevitable product of the technological revolution is an authoritarian state. This assumption undergirded the political philosophy of Lenin, Mussolini, Hitler, and others.

What has actually happened, however, is that while government has become larger and more complex, it also has become more decentralized. The relatively rapid growth in the number of persons employed by and in the expenditures of state and local governments is but one sign of this decentralization.

It is difficult to overstate the importance of this continued diffusion of power to the change-oriented person. It raises three basic issues. First, does he agree this is the dominant basic long-term trend? Unless he agrees this is a reasonable

**155**

representation of reality, he will not be influenced by it.

Second, assuming he believes this is the basic long-range trend, what does this say to his strategy for change? Will he concentrate on attacking the establishment? On helping to continue this diffusion of power? Or will he try to achieve a redistribution—rather than a continued diffusion—of power? Or will he focus his attention on building new coalitions that will have the combined power (hopefully) to promote and implement change? These are substantially differing goals and the appropriate strategy is influenced by the goal selected.

Contrary to the conventional wisdom of the day, there is substantial evidence to support the suggestion that the pace of change today is slower than desired by many, not because of the opposition of a malevolent power bloc, but primarily because power is so diffused that while the number of persons and groups with a veto power has grown, there are fewer and fewer with sufficient power to cause a major change in the direction of events. This can be seen in such varied issues as the growing problems of water pollution, the unacceptable level of unemployment, the shortage of electric power, the economic drain on society by organized crime, the annual toll of automobile deaths, the continued existence of white racism, the decline of mass transit, the disappearance of the family farm, and the increasing contamination of the air. Where is sufficient power lodged in one place in American society to sharply alter any one of those conditions?

An acceptance of this thesis raises the third issue. It suggests the change-oriented person has only two alternatives in regard to the continued dispersion of power. On the one hand, he can oppose any further diffusion of power and seek to build up a strong central focal point for power. This has been the traditional position of the political liberal on the issue of states' rights versus the increase in the power of a strong central government. The local parallel for this has been the liberal support for metropolitan government as one means of solving the problems created by the combination of the fragmentation of local government and urban sprawl.

The other alternative is to accept, favor, and support the continued dispersal of power, the multiplication of separate power centers, and the increasing complexity of the decision-making process.[17] This means any change from the status quo can be accomplished most effectively by the normally slow and laborious process of coalition building.

## The Ethical and Moral Dilemma

This brings into focus the ethical and moral dilemma of the change-oriented individual. Does he favor increasing the pace of change or the continued dispersal of power?

This immediately raises the issue of criteria. What are the criteria for making this choice? The classic criteria used by Christians in responding to the use of power include neighbor-centered love, the goal of love and justice, a continued concern that the end sought does not subvert the means used to reach that end, and the concept of mutual forgiveness based on reuniting love as the fulfillment of creative justice.

As scores of committed Christian scholars have demonstrated, there are no easy or simple answers to this dilemma.[18]

There are ethical, moral, and religious dimensions to the use of power. The Christian has given to him some absolutes which, as a Christian, he accepts by definition. He has some guidelines in the nature of power which enable him to predict what probably will happen in a given set of circumstances, and this enables him to act accordingly. For example, there is the issue of accountability. By definition, a Christian believes each person is accountable for his actions. Therefore, the Christian will consistently favor the dispersion or redistribution of power in a process which maximizes the degree of accountability and sharpens the lines of accountability, rather than a diffusion of power through a process which blurs or erases the lines of accountability.

It is in this direction, rather than in the direction of increasing the number of simple, rigid, and external rules, that the Christian must look as he contemplates the issues of conflict and controversy in the process of planned social change.

# 6

# Anticipating and Managing Conflict

In looking at the 1968 elections, pollster Louis Harris suggested the nation was in the middle of a major political realignment. For years, perhaps for as long as nine decades, the political divisions had tended to follow economic lines. In looking at the contemporary scene, Harris pointed to the emergence of two new coalitions, one advocating change and the other opposing change. In the coalition composed of persons and groups opposing change, Harris listed whites in the Deep South, older people, conservative suburbanites, and low-middle-income whites in the northern industrial cities. In the coalition favoring change, Harris included Negroes, Spanish-speaking people, Jews, the young, the affluent, and many of the college-educated people in the population.[1]

In recent years the Gallup Poll has asked a sample of the American population how they felt about the churches' involvement in political and social matters. In 1957, 44 percent of those interviewed wanted the churches to keep out of those issues. Eleven years later, this figure had jumped to 53 percent.[2]

In a widely reported address to Americans for Democratic Action (ADA) back in September, 1967, Daniel Patrick Moynihan suggested that increasingly liberals would recognize "their essential interest is in the stability of the social order, and that given the present threats to that stability, it is necessary to seek out and make much more effective alliances with political conservatives who share that concern." While subsequent events proved this suggestion to be an accurate prediction, at the time Moynihan was attacked by a variety of leaders from the left for legitimatizing a liberal-conservative alliance.

These three incidents illustrate one of the most important dimensions of planned social change. Controversy and conflict are unavoidable. They are an inseparable part of the process of intentional, internally motivated, social change-points of conflict.

It may be helpful for the advocate of change to be aware of a few of these major points of conflict.

One of the most obvious is illustrated by Lou Harris' definition of the new political realignment. The same division can be seen in other segments of society where the proponents of change and the opponents form two distinctly separate blocs. This division can be seen in the legal profession between the advocates and opponents of "no-fault" automobile insurance, in the black community between the proponents and opponents of racial integration, in the medical profession between those favoring and those opposing publicly financed, universal medical coverage, in the Roman Catholic Church between those for and those against a change in the rule of celibacy for priests, in South America between those supporting a ban on the use of DDT and those opposing such a ban, and in the building trades union between the proponents of a change in the entrance requirements and those opposing such changes.

While the conflict appears to be over the immediate issue, in larger terms it is over change and the anticipated consequences of change.

Perhaps the most consistent and recurring point of conflict is over the definition of purpose. This point of conflict was illustrated by the Gallup Poll on whether the churches should be involved in social and political issues. This conflict often is concealed, intentionally or accidentally, until a change from the status quo is proposed. Not infrequently members of an organization who differ on a definition of purpose can unite on a specific project which appears to be a means of improving the capability of the organization to fulfill its purpose. The conflict over definition of purpose does not become apparent until the emphasis shifts from getting ready to going into action.

One example of this is the voluntary association that unites to raise money, and then divides over how it should be spent. Another is the series of community action groups that were organized in the 1960s, first in response to the war on poverty and later in response to the Model Cities program. Was their purpose to *advise* the local public agencies or to *control* the policy formulation process? A

161

third example is illustrated by the Hale's Corners Church described in the next chapter.

Another common point of conflict is illustrated by Moynihan's suggestion that liberals and conservatives band together to maintain the stability of the social order. To some liberal and radical proponents of change this suggestion of an alliance with conservatives was heretical. This illustrates the conflict over allies. As soon as the advocates of intentional change reach that point when it becomes necessary to build a supporting group, this issue often rises to the surface. Who are the "proper" potential allies? Frequently the division on this point of conflict parallels the division between those who are primarily interested in a prophetic witness and those who are primarily interested in change. This division often produces the same groupings that can be seen in the split between the radical revolutionaries and the liberal reformers or between those who are primarily against the status quo and those who are primarily for implementation of a new vision.

A fourth point of conflict in the change process that is closely related to the last two is over compromise and the acceptability of proximate goals. Adherents to the teachings of the late Reinhold Niebuhr and his concept of Christian realism will have less difficulty accepting the inevitability of compromise than will those who act from a different philosophical base.

Another common point of conflict that has not received adequate attention in recent discussions on planned change is the question of authority. Ever since the Students for a Democratic Society (SDS) came forth with their now famous Port Huron Statement in 1962, the discontent with the degree of political democratization in the United States has been climbing. Much of the public discussion has been devoted to the concept of "participatory democracy," to the democratization of other social institutions (family, schools, corporations, churches, etc.) in which power is distributed even more unevenly than in the state, and to the challenge to authority.

Comparatively little attention has been directed to the basis for authority. In a brilliantly written little book Robert A. Dahl has suggested three criteria for evaluating the validity of the decision-making process in terms of authority. These are: (1) the degree to which the decisions coincide with my personal choice, (2) the necessity for specialized competence, and (3) economy of time, attention, and energy.[3] These three criteria offer the agent of change a very useful rational framework for resolving conflict over authority. Later Dahl goes back to Rousseau's *Social Contract* as a base for examining the limitations in the concept of participatory democracy.

Another very helpful frame of reference for examining conflicts over authority is offered by Roger L. Shinn as he examines the growing conflict between the authority of the technological expert and that of the man in the street.[4]

Shinn also discusses the challenge of participatory democracy to expert authority and offers a very useful outline for keeping expert authority subject to a critical review without moving either to anarchy or to the dangerous elitism that has dominated much of the philosophical expression of the New Left.

Still another point of conflict that is becoming increasingly visible is over leadership styles. As was pointed out in

Chapter 4, "Big Daddy" is dead, but not every advocate of change believes that. Frequently the person who is perceived as the key leader in the change process is viewed as the "wrong" type or style of leader by other members of the initiating group and by potential members of the supporting group. In some situations he is viewed as too authoritarian, in others as too nondirective, and occasionally as overly concerned with a collaborative approach to decision-making.

Closely related to this is another point of conflict and one which is often very deceptive. This is the conflict of personalities. There is a natural tendency among sinful human beings to blame the other guy for whatever goes wrong. This is perceived as a clash of personalities and often produces or intensifies conflicts between or among individuals. This can and often does paralyze the whole effort at planned change.

During the past two decades tremendous progress has been made at identifying, isolating, and resolving conflict which is primarily a conflict of personalities.

On the other hand, there is also the risk that viewing conflict in only psychological terms can obscure, rather than reveal, basic conflicts over administrative styles, philosophical positions, or definitions of purposes. Attempts to deal with only one can obscure the others.

Finally there is a broad area of conflict in the change process which includes several specific points of tension and conflict. These can be grouped under the broad umbrella of philosophy or ideology and include the ends versus means issue, the conflicts over tactics, ethical and moral questions, and probable consequences.

An example of this is the interpretation of the New Left's

philosophy that is offered by many liberals over thirty years of age. These older liberals have a very serious conflict with the New Left which is becoming increasingly apparent. One dimension of this is the belief that like all other revolutionaries, the radical revolutionaries on the New Left are attempting to impose a single ideological framework on a highly complex, pragmatic, and pluralistic process of decision-making in the United States today. This means there is a conflict over the definition of reality, over the philosophical base for analyzing problems, over the appropriate tactics, over the probable consequences of the course of action advocated by any one faction of the New Left, and over the place of moral and ethical values as well as over those values.

One result is conflict with a relatively low level of productivity, partly because of the failure to identify a common agenda. This brings up two questions. The first is how to respond to conflict. American society is filled with conflict and with a tremendous variety of responses to conflict. The most widely used include the marketplace, referral to a committee, exercising the right of withdrawal, bribes, legislative bodies, elections, the budgeting process,[5] referenda, confrontation, redundancy, strikes, tantrums, negotiating teams, sanctions, tears, compromise, money, precedent, indecision, the use of a small executive committee, and the delegation of authority to a chief executive officer. What does the agent of change with an intentional anticipatory style of leadership see as the most productive response to conflict? What is his "style" for resolving conflict? Obviously the "right" answer will vary with the situation and the individual.

The second question is, How can the anticipatory style leader exploit an understanding of the potential points of conflicts in his efforts to facilitate change?

## A Constructive Approach

If the change agent is able to look at the process of planned social change and see the many points of potential conflict, this can offer him several benefits. The acceptance of that suggestion can be seen most clearly in the tremendous recent increase in the use of case studies, role play, simulation exercises as training aids, and game theory.[6] They are one method for anticipating conflicts and other difficulties. These devices also are one of the symbolic marks of the emergence of an anticipatory style of leadership in many segments of American society.

The first point in looking forward to or anticipating possible points of conflict is the vast difference between looking forward to conflict and anticipating conflict as a normal and natural part of the process of planned social change. Too often conflict is feared and avoided, thus inhibiting the entire process.

Second, if anticipated, it is possible to keep conflict from becoming such a diversion that it halts the planning process and makes planned change impossible. There are many methods for managing conflict. These include such common items as laws, rules of procedure, an agenda, voting, and a range of training programs developed by behavioral scientists. The person who knows the points of probable conflict in the change process can utilize these to manage the inevitable conflict in a creative manner. It also has been suggested that effective conflict management can reduce the apparent suddenness of change and encourage a less disruptive gradual change.[7]

The advocate of change who can anticipate conflict also is better prepared to distinguish between surface symptoms and the real hurts in the change process. At a time of conflict the symptoms often have high visibility and they may conceal the basic hurt. The most obvious example of this is the person who bursts into tears during a moment of stress at one of the points of conflict in the change process. The tears can be stopped, but little is accomplished unless the cause for the crying is discovered.

One of the most important phenomena of the change process is that points of conflicts also often become points of great creativity. The nature of the conflict that often accompanies change frequently provides a far more fertile climate for creativity than does the rigidity which sometimes is a part of orderliness.[8] Conflict can help improve communication, prevent polarization, and shift the balance of power in an organization. The advocate of change who can anticipate conflict may be better prepared to exploit this potential creativity.

Perhaps the most important reason for encouraging the change agent to be able to anticipate the points of potential conflict is that this will help him to be prepared to help set the limits for permissible conflict. While conflict is inevitable in the internally motivated process of intentional social change, and while conflict can be creative, conflict always carries a price tag and the price can escalate very suddenly and very rapidly. Thus by being prepared, the advocate of change can reduce the possibilities of conflict being a complete diversion from change or from becoming an end in itself.[9]

An essential element of any effective effort to manage conflict constructively is the ability to perceive a cycle or predictable pattern of conflict. Being able to recognize this pattern is one of the marks of anticipatory leadership. One researcher has suggested that the cycle usually begins with a single issue, which disrupts ("unfreezes") the equilibrium. Following this, previously suppressed issues begin to appear and the beliefs of the opponent are brought into the disagreement until it is easy to perceive the opponent as totally bad or completely wrong. This leads into the leveling of charges against the opponent as a person, and before long the dispute is removed from the original basis of disagreement.[10]

The advocate of change who is able to anticipate conflict also may be able to prevent the polarization which can immobilize an organization. Polarization usually is the result of a series of conflicts which consistently divide members of the group along the same lines. Once this pattern has been established, there is a tendency for people automatically to divide along the same lines, especially when the conflict cycle moves quickly to personalities. One dimension of the constructive management of conflict is to keep the division on issues, not personalities. As this happens repeatedly during the process of planned change, allies at one point become opponents at another, and opponents at one point of conflict become allies at a subsequent point. This is one of the most effective means of preventing the polarization of a group along the same cleavage, thus enabling the process of planned change to continue.

One approach to planned change is to anticipate the points of conflict and to resolve these conflicts in a manner that facilitates the process of change. A related approach is to prevent polarization.

## Preventing Polarization

The point has been made repeatedly in the preceding pages that conflict is an integral part of the process of planned social change and that conflict can be a creative part of the entire process. When conflict leads to polarization, however, it tends to either halt or divert the process of intentional change. The person who is primarily concerned with a prophetic witness may find polarization to be a useful ally. The advocate of planned change, however, will find polarization a barrier to achievement of his goals and the anticipatory style of change-agent leadership will seek to prevent polarization. These ten rules have been used by church leaders in their efforts to prevent the polarization that paralyzes:

1. Keep the channels of communication open. The best illustration of this is the process of writing a treaty between two conflicting parties.

2. Depersonalize dissent. One of the most frequent causes of the termination of communication is that the argument used to criticize an individual's proposal, program, or position is regarded by him as a personal attack. Two of the best illustrations of how this can be avoided can be seen in the procedures governing debate in the United States Senate and the format for handling dissent in the U. S. Supreme Court.

3. Try to look inside the other person's frame of reference. There is an old saying about walking in another man's shoes. There is an important truth in this conventional wisdom, and it often is very helpful to try to look at the issue from the perspective of another party in the conflict. Role playing in race relations is an excellent illustration of this approach.

4. Open the door to creative *and* meaningful participation by every person. This is especially useful in the local church. When one person is encouraged to maximize his positive contributions and to utilize his talents and skills in the life, ministry, and outreach of the congregation, he usually is much more open to the idea that others may hear a different call and be drawn to a different response.

5. Keep opening new opportunities for people to invest themselves in service and ministry. As a person gives of himself, he tends to grow, and as he grows, this opens up additional opportunities.

A simple illustration of the application of this is the common rule that no one can hold the same office in the local church for more than three or four years or the same office in the denomination for more than eight years.

6. Seek agreement on short-term or intermediate goals. Too often the cause of unnecessary conflict and the emergence of the type of polarization that immobilizes is the focus on ultimate goals. Again, the conventional wisdom that points out the longest journey begins with a single step is applicable.

7. Study the twelfth chapter of Paul's first letter to the church at Corinth. A recognition of the diversity of min-

istries is an essential element in effectively overcoming the paralysis of polarization.

8. Build a sense of mutual trust within the organization. This is one of the most important possibilities. When people trust one another, there is almost no limit on what can happen. Where this mutual trust exists, dissent and confrontation can be very creative forces.

An outstanding negative illustration of this is in those many congregations where adults are unwilling to trust the capabilities of young persons, and young people distrust the motivations and goals of older persons. In these congregations attempts at a creative ministry to *and by* young persons have been wrecked on the rocks of mutual distrust.

9. For the denominational judicatory such as the conference, synod, association, district, or presbytery, a useful method for improving communication, reducing misunderstandings, and eliminating some of the negative effects of polarization is to formally establish a grievance committee *which will hold hearings on a regularly scheduled basis throughout the judicatory.*

10. Recognize the events and factors that produce a paralyzing effect. One of the most widespread illustrations of this is the deliberate escalation of rhetoric. As voices become louder, as assertions become more categorical, and as descriptive terms become extreme, the quality of communication declines and the possibilities for polarization rise.

While these suggestions for anticipating and managing conflict and for preventing polarization have been drawn from the experiences of both effective change agents and the observations of students of social change, they do have one limitation.

That limitation is expressed in the response of the great football coach Knute Rockne, who was asked why he allowed the scouts from future opponents to visit football practice at Notre Dame. Wasn't he afraid they would steal the plays? He replied, "It isn't the play that wins the game. It's the execution." So it is with the constructive management of conflict.

# 7

# Organizational Change

When John F. Kennedy was elected President in 1960, he was determined to restore the State Department to its historic position as the focal point for the conduct of foreign affairs. Immediately after his election he established a special task force to study the problem. Kennedy also recognized the critical importance of his appointments at both the cabinet and subcabinet level in any effort to revitalize the Department.

Yet within six months after his inauguration he was saying that sending an instruction to the State Department was "like dropping it in the dead-letter box" and "the State Department is a bowl of jelly." [1] Within a year after his election the new President felt obligated to initiate major personnel changes in what became known as "the Thanksgiving Massacre of 1961." [2]

In 1963 when W. Averell Harriman was appointed as Undersecretary for Political Affairs it was hoped this might help the State Department become once again a positive and creative force in world affairs. This, too, was an illusion. The State Department continued through the Kennedy, Johnson, and Nixon years to become increasingly irrelevant despite the efforts of each President to restore it to its former effectiveness. [3]

The Hale's Corners Church was founded in 1841 at a crossroads community which included a blacksmith shop, a post office in the general store, and a tavern which served as an overnight stop on the stagecoach runs. In 1900 the congregation included 113 members. By 1955 this figure had increased to 117, of whom 103 lived on farms. In 1964, with the opening of the new highway a mile away, Hale's Corners was beginning to look more like a suburban community and the membership of the church had more than doubled to 243. With the vigorous encouragement of the denomination the congregation began to plan for the future, and what appeared to be the critical decision was made at a special congregational meeting in 1965 when the members voted 116 to 23 in favor of a plan to build an $85,000 two-story masonry structure on the four-acre site which included a small cemetery and the seventy-year-old white frame church building. It was assumed that when the new structure was completed, the old structure would be razed.

By 1971 the number of residents in the township was double the 1965 figure; the new church building had been completed and paid for; the membership total stood at 219;

the man who had been the pastor from 1959 to 1966 had left the ministry and was selling insurance; his successor, who came directly from seminary, served from 1966 to 1969 and then left the professional ministry to teach school; and in 1971 his thirty-one-year-old successor was contemplating leaving the ministry and going to law school.

The frustrations recent Presidents have experienced with the State Department and the unexpected failure of the Hale's Corners Church to grow with the urbanization of that community both illustrate one of the most subtle issues facing anyone concerned with planned change.

Unless there is a change in the direction, value system, and orientation of the organization, frequently there are severe limitations on what can be accomplished by changes in people or by the addition of new personnel. This phenomenon is illustrated by the comparatively minor impact a succession of new faces in the top-policy positions have had on the functioning of the State Department.

A recent critic of what is sometimes referred to as "The Great Wind Machine" argues there can be no significant change in American foreign policy until after there have been major changes made in the organizational structure and in the direction, value system, and orientation of the many agencies now involved in policy formation and execution.[4]

This same point is also illustrated by the Hale's Corners Church where, despite an influx of new members, a new building program, and a succession of future-oriented ministers, the congregation continues to act on the assumption that this is a small rural church where institutional survival is the most important factor to be considered in making

175

policy decisions. The newcomers to Hale's Corners who were comfortable with this perspective encountered few difficulties in being assimilated into the life of this fellowship. Most of the old-timers and nearly all of the newcomers could unite around a building program since the construction symbolized different values and different dreams to different persons.

After the new structure was completed, however, the difference in values and in definition of purpose became more visible. Those with a future orientation who saw the new structure as a tool of ministry and who emphasized the necessity of enlarging and diversifying the program to reach and serve more of the new residents moving out to Hale's Corners soon realized they were a small, powerless, and ineffectual minority. The majority, which included most of the old-timers and a large proportion of the newer members, continued to give a higher priority to survival goals and to institutional maintenance than to mission and service. A symbolic event in this struggle occurred in 1968 when the church council accepted the recommendation of the trustees that the Friday-night teen-age club be discontinued because of $183 damage in the form of broken windows, flooded rest rooms, and broken chairs during the first year of the club's existence.

All three of the pastors, both of the denominational executives, and a church-planning consultant who had worked with the Hale's Corners Church during this period were misled by the early ease which this congregation displayed in receiving and assimilating newcomers and by the enthusiastic support that had been given to the building program. Much later they realized they had misinterpreted support for strengthening the institution as an openness to change.

This same pattern of behavior can be observed in many places besides the State Department and the small rural congregation in an urbanizing community. It can be seen in the business firm which sends several key executives to T-groups, sensitivity training labs, and other personal growth experiences. They come back with a new perspective, a changed value system, and lots of optimism about what can be done to create a smoother functioning and more productive organization. But they also come back to the same old organization largely filled with the same old faces, adhering to the same old value system, being guided by the same old policies in making the same old decisions, and headed in the same old direction.

This pattern can be seen in the public school system where a few venturesome persons go out and catch a vision of how exciting the educational process could be. They may even bring back a working model of how to reach this goal. But they, too, come back to the same old school system they had left which is still controlled by the same old value system and headed in the same old direction.

This same pattern can be seen in the frequent frustrations encountered by the reformer who joins one of the major political parties, in the growing disillusionment of the couple who return from an inspiring week-long retreat with a new vision of the church to find their congregation dedicated to continuing to do business as usual, and in the disappointments of the person who reluctantly accepts election to a high and important office, not because he wants to trade personal privacy and freedom for prestige and status, but because he is convinced he has an obligation to change the style of leadership in that organization.

This same pattern can be seen in the experiences of the young and bright-eyed graduate who goes out with a master's or doctor's degree from a school of social work or a theological seminary or a law school or a graduate school of business or public administration to instill new ideas into his new profession and to sharply upgrade the performance of that profession.

In each of these illustrations the return from the dream of what tomorrow could be to the facts of what yesterday was and still is tends to be a disillusioning and sometimes a shattering personal experience for the change-oriented individual.

## Why?

The answer to that complex one-word question lies in what Peter Drucker identified in 1954 as "the new reality." Drucker argued that the old view of the old world, the old slogans, and the old approaches to problem solving no longer make sense. In the new reality a new approach is needed. Nowhere is this more apparent than in organizations, and especially in organizations confronted with the pressure of change.[5]

In the old reality the expression "a new broom sweeps clean" frequently was a relevant descriptive term for what happened when new leadership came into an organization. The new leadership often changed the organization. A new president of a corporation or a new mayor of a city or a new pastor for a congregation or a new superintendent for the local school system or a new secretary for a federal department or a new president for a college frequently meant significant changes in the performance of that organization that soon had a high degree of visibility.

In the new reality, to use the same analogy, "a new broom is soon worn out." The direction and the performance of the organization continue much as in the past as people come and go. Whether the reason is described as organizational inertia or institutional blight or simply as the nature of organizations, it is increasingly difficult for a change in personnel or even a change within the people themselves to influence the attitude and performance of the organization.

In response to the new reality a new discipline has emerged called "organization development." [6] The central element in the theory and practice of organization development is to improve the capability of an organization to identify and evaluate alternative courses of action. This means freeing the organization from the tyranny of precedent.

This usually requires a reexamination of the definition of purpose, of the value system that controls the decision-making process, and the charting of a new direction for the organization. Frequently this process reveals that the original direction of the organization has been subverted in one of two ways. Either what had been developed as a means to reach a goal had become the goal itself, or the original goal had been replaced by a goal of institutional maintenance and survival.

The reasons for this subversion of goals are many and varied, but they can be summarized in one word—change. This means the contemporary advocate of intentional change

179

is faced with the choice of mastering the fundamentals of organization development or of experiencing the frustrations John F. Kennedy had with the State Department and a series of people encountered in working with the Hale's Corners Church.

The emergence of the new reality and the resulting demand for this discipline called organization development can be described in several ways.

Samuel Lubell has identified as "the hidden crisis in American politics" a departure from what he has labeled "the old politics of stability." Lubell describes eight points at which contemporary conditions vary from the old pattern or the old reality.[7] One of these is the attack on a whole range of institutions such as the public schools, the churches, the welfare system, the military establishment, the draft, the police, the universities, the political parties, the hospitals, the prisons, and several of the large business corporations. One of the reasons for these attacks has been the inability (which is perceived as unwillingness) of these institutions and organizations to respond to the pressures of rapid social change.

Another perspective on the situation can be seen by comparing the nature of federal responses to what were perceived as national problems in the 1930s with the responses of the last fifteen or twenty years. The New Deal produced a series of programs which were relatively simple and easy to implement. The federal insurance of bank deposits, Old Age and Survivor's insurance (Social Security), price supports for farmers, and special benefits for farmers are representative examples. There were a few attempts to change the social patterns of American life, such as the Aid to

Dependent Children program to keep mother and child together and a tiny program to resettle people on farms.

Beginning in 1954 with the school desegregation decision by the United States Supreme Court there have been a series of actions by the Federal Government to change human institutions and to change behavior patterns. These include financial inducements for young people to study science and engineering (a radically different concept than the G. I. Bill, which simply encouraged veterans to attend college), the desegregation of residential communities, an emphasis on performance and quality rather than activities and quantity in evaluating public education, encouraging people to move out of the city to the suburbs, subsidizing the fragmentation of local government, treating (as contrasted with simply disposing) of sewage and garbage, offering financial inducements for communities to plan for the future, encouraging the development of new channels for citizen participation in community decision-making, making English the universal language in the United States, subsidizing mid-career changes in vocations, encouraging people to limit the size of their families, reducing the risk of death or injury on the highways, and encouraging people to switch from rail to highway or air travel for long-distance trips. In each one of these programs the emphasis is on change rather than on stability.

In perhaps one-half of these programs the performance approached or even exceeded the expectations. In the other half, however, the rhetoric greatly exceeded the performance. When the newly created expectations were not fulfilled, people naturally began to ask why not. One of the explanations was that "the system" was unresponsive to the demands for change. This was obviously true, but again came that one-word question: Why? It soon became apparent that it was much easier for a person to change his attitudes, his expectations, his values, or his destination than it was for "the system" to make the necessary changes. As people perceived that when a new leader was placed in charge of an organization it tended to be the leader and not the organization that changed, there emerged a new discipline to determine not only why that tended to be the pattern, but what could be done about it.

Out of this came the diagnosis that the traditional bureaucratic structure combined with an increasing size and complexity in organizations plus the diffusion of power in American society and a new emphasis on the importance of human relations made it impossible for the typical organization to respond effectively to the pressures of rapid social change, the demand for broader participation, and an increasing degree of diversity in society.[8]

## What?

The change agent who recognizes that he is functioning in a society filled with institutions and dominated by the interaction of institutions can understand the need to change the behavior of institutions. It is not sufficient to concentrate on changing the behavior of individuals. It also is necessary to change the behavior of institutions and organizations. Organization development (OD) is one approach to that task.

Organization development is a deliberate effort to improve the effectiveness of an organization by planned intervention in the behavior patterns of the total system (or organization). Almost invariably this requires not only the knowledge and approval of the top echelon of policy-makers in the organization, it also requires their active participation. Normally the effort requires two to four years for the desired changes to be accomplished. One by-product of that characteristic is that many OD efforts are undercut by (a) the short-term system of evaluation and reward that is an integral element of most organizations (the annual report is an obvious example) and (b) the turnover in personnel.

Organization development is designed to improve the health of an organization and to increase the capability of the organization to achieve its goals.[9] This means goals rather than roles, collaboration rather than competition, and ideas rather than personalities are emphasized in the decision-making process. In brief, it is an effort to help an organization develop its own capacity for "self-renewal," to use John Gardner's phrase.[10] It is an attempt, usually assisted by an outside change agent consultant, to help the people within the organization "perceive, understand, and act upon process events" in the functioning of that organization.[11]

Organization development is a response to change, it includes a strategy for planned change, and the primary focus is on the human side of the enterprise.

To go back to the beginning of this chapter, it is a means of helping the people in the State Department and in the Hale's Corners congregation to understand their situations more clearly, to enable them to work out a more effective means of defining their contemporary goals, to examine their present operations against these goals, and to develop a more effective means for accomplishing those goals.

## How?

The strategies used in organization development vary with the circumstances and the consultant. One approach can be illustrated by a page from a denominational report on Christian education which described the presuppositions it found to be operative in the educational program of many congregations:

1. The provision of a Sunday church school for the childhood years of a person's life is normative and adequate.
2. The middle- or early-teen years are the terminal point in church education.
3. A maximum of sixty minutes once a week for seven or eight months in the year is adequate time.
4. No significant investment needs to be made by the congregation in the training of teachers or in providing resources for learning.
5. Standards and goals for evaluating learning experiences or effective teaching are not important or necessary.
6. The Sunday church school does not need to have any integral and continuing relationship to the life of worship, fellowship, and service of the congregation.[12]

These were *not* the recommended standards. These were what were perceived as the presuppositions which, judged from outward appearances, did control the educational program in many congregations.

The strategy here was to help members of the organization (in this case local churches) identify the discrepancy between their conception of what constituted the presuppositions underlying their program and what outsiders saw as reality.

One of the most common OD strategies is based on the assumption that an organization functions around teams (groups) rather than individuals, and therefore high priority should be given to team building.[13]

Other strategies focus on goal setting, on the assumption that an organization functions in the context of goals; on intergroup relations and conflict;[14] on internal communication within an organization;[15] on the "needs" or "satisfactions" of members of the organization;[16] on the organization of work; or on the internal environment.

## But!

There are four dimensions to organization development that may be overlooked by change agents. The first, and perhaps the most difficult, is to understand the functioning and the dynamics of the organization. The older the organization or the system, the more difficult it often is to understand the contemporary functions of the organization.

Perhaps the outstanding contemporary illustration of this has been the repeated attempts in recent years to reform the welfare system. Thus far these efforts have failed. One reason is they have failed to change the values of the system—and this cannot be accomplished unless the functions of the system are thoroughly and accurately perceived. In recent years the welfare system in the United States has become increasingly oriented to dislocation in the work system and to the maintenance of civil order.[17] Until these functions of the welfare system are recognized, it is unrealistic to expect even the most dedicated change agents to be successful in reforming the system and making it more responsive to the needs of the poor. As long as the efforts at change are based on a perception of the welfare system as *primarily* a relief-giving operation, these efforts are doomed to failure, regardless of how sensitive the change agents may be to people and to people's needs. Especially vulnerable are any efforts at change based on a strategy of goal setting or on team building.

In other words, the desired changes in an organization are not likely to be achieved, regardless of the strategy of change, unless people perceive what are the actual operative goals of the organization or system.

A second caution grows out of the fact that very few organizations function in a vacuum. Most organizations are part of a system which is part of a larger system, which in turn is part of a still larger system, and so on. Unless the entire system is changed, there is a limit to the changes that can be accomplished and accommodated in any one part of the total system.

One example of this is the difficulty encountered by President Richard Nixon's proposal to reorganize his cabinet and the federal bureaucracy.[18] Another example is the newly elected bishop who decided that his would be a "new style" of episcopal leadership—and he found that major changes were necessary in the denominational structure before he could implement his plans for a new style of leadership for either himself or his colleagues.

A third dimension that is entirely consistent with the basic presuppositions of organization development, but tends to be overlooked by both consultants and clients, is the general principle that an increase in complexity creates a greater demand for democracy—and often makes possible a greater degree of democracy than many people perceive. There is a general tendency to "favor democratic procedures, but in this case it's too difficult or time-consuming or the issues are too complex." [19]

The scientific revolution is widening the gap between conventional political wisdom and expert knowledge. The more complex the problem, the more likely that the intuitive answer will be the wrong answer, and perhaps even counterproductive. Perhaps the only way open today to bridge that gap is to increase the degree of participatory democracy and to reduce the power of the expert or of the top-echelon bureaucrat. One means of achieving that which has been largely neglected outside local government is referendum democracy. While this has and undoubtedly will continue to produce some conservative decisions, the implications for change are less severe than those which accompany a widening of the gap between the expert and the people.

A greater dependence on referendum democracy may become one of the most useful tools in the efforts to change the direction or orientation of organizations.

Finally, many organizations have tried to alter their direction with only a partial approach to change. In the State Department a change of top leadership was not sufficient. At the Hale's Corners Church a change in pastors did not change the direction of the organization. The limited effectiveness of goal-setting strategies in organizational change has demonstrated that sometimes it too is inadequate by itself. Occasionally there must be *both* changes in the organization's behavior *and* changes of personnel if the direction of an organization is to be altered and if its health and effectiveness are to be improved.

A recent example of this was the public school system in Philadelphia, which was established in 1818 to serve the children of the poor. (The upper classes sent their children to private schools operated by the Quakers and Episcopalians.) By 1965 it was clear the system was not serving its clientele adequately, and a new school board was appointed and began to change the system. By 1967 it was apparent that the changes in the system introduced by the new school board were not adequate, and a new superintendent, Mark Shedd, was secured. While the reform of the Philadelphia schools is not complete, it could never have gone as far as it has without changing both the functioning of the organization and also replacing personnel.[20]

The insights and skills that are a part of organization development theory are an essential part of the equipment of the person who expects to be a responsible and effective agent of change in what is becoming an increasingly complex society.

# Notes

## Chapter 1: How to Cut Your Own Throat

1. A case study approach to the problems encountered by organizers of the poor and of the dangers they must avoid to be effective can be found in Harry Brill, *Why Organizers Fail* (Berkeley: University of California Press, 1971). This account of a militant effort to organize a rent strike among residents of a public housing project is filled with perceptive insights for the contemporary change agent. For a look at the change process from a perspective that contrasts the conflict approach to change and the evolutionary process, see Kenneth Boulding, *A Primer on Social Dynamics* (New York: The Free Press, 1970). Boulding comes out clearly on the side of the nondialectical approach.

## Chapter 2: The Nature of Change

1. "Poverty Increases by 1.2 Million in 1970," United States Department of Commerce *Current Population Reports*, Series P-60, No. 77, May 7, 1971.

2. Henry Bienen, *Violence and Social Change: A Review of Current Literature* (Chicago: University of Chicago Press, 1968), p. 2. A useful general introduction to the subject is Amitai Etzioni and Eva Etzioni, eds., *Social Change* (New York: Basic Books, 1964).

3. Thomas R. Bennett II, *The Leader and the Process of Planned Change* (New York: Association Press, 1962), pp. 21-27. This little cartoon-filled, 63-page booklet is an exceptionally brief and lucid introduction to the whole subject of planned social change.

4. Kurt Lewin, *Resolving Social Conflicts*, ed. Gertrud Weiss Lewin and Gordon W. Allport (New York: Harper & Brothers, 1948), pp. 56-57.

5. Wilbert E. Moore, *Social Change* (Englewood Cliffs, N.J.: Prentice-Hall, 1963), p. 2.

6. One dimension of this conflict is the differences in perspective. An excellent recent book to test the differences in perception of reality is Charles A. Reich, *The Greening of America* (New York: Random House, 1970). As with the record album "Jesus Christ Superstar," the reactions to the message are more revealing than the contents.

7. Robert Bendiner, *New York Times Magazine*, February 4, 1968, p. 71. For a scholarly analysis of how the anarchy that recently has been labeled revolution actually impedes the process of change, see Benjamin R. Barber, *Superman and Common Men* (New York: Praeger, 1971). For a tragic example of what may happen when the rhetoric is escalated to the point that it distorts communication, see Paul Goodman's letter to the editors of the *New York Review of Books*, October 21, 1971, p. 54. Goodman contends that in the Attica prison riot the prisoners' threat to cut the throats of the hostages was symbolic language and should not have been construed literally by Governor Rockefeller or Commissioner Oswald.

8. Peter Drucker, *Landmarks of Tomorrow* (New York: Harper & Row, 1959), pp. 46-50.

9. For a discussion of the favorable climate for innovation, see Donald A. Schon, *Technology and Change* (New York: Delacorte Press, 1967), pp. 172-77, and Lyle E. Schaller, *Parish Planning* (Nashville: Abingdon Press, 1971), pp. 75-88. A more generalized discussion of innovation is found in Horace M. Kallen, "Innovation," in *Social Change*, ed. Etzioni and Etzioni. A useful collection of essays on innovation and creativity directed at the business leader but also of relevance for the change agent can

be found in Gary A. Steiner, ed., *The Creative Organization* (Chicago: The University of Chicago Press, 1971). An example of how a timely attempt at forced innovation failed is described by Dorothy Nelkin, *The Politics of Housing Innovation* (Ithaca: Cornell University Press, 1971). This case study illustrates the problems encountered in transferring skills and insights from object-centered research and technology to the solution of person-centered social problems.

10. Several on this list of twelve characteristics of the creative organization are adapted from Frieda B. Libaw, "And Now, the Creative Corporation," *Innovation*, March, 1971, pp. 2-13.

11. Quoted in Charles Judah and George Winston Smith, *The Unchosen* (New York: Coward-McCann, 1962), p. 277.

12. "Teaching German," *School Review*, June, 1918, pp. 458-59.

13. Frantz Fanon, *Black Skins, White Masks* (New York: Grove Press, 1967); Harvey Pressman, "Schools to Beat the System" *Psychology Today*, March, 1969, pp. 58-63; Jonathan Kozol, *Death at an Early Age* (Boston: Houghton Mifflin, 1967); Mary Frances Greene, *The School Children: Growing Up in the Slums* (New York: New American Library, 1967); Robert C. Maynard, "Black Nationalism and Community Schools"; Henry M. Levin, *Community Control of Schools* (Washington, D.C.: The Brookings Institution, 1970).

14. Adam Yarmolinsky, *The Military Establishment* (New York: Harper & Row, 1971), pp. 324-29.

15. For a brief introduction to the subject of expectations, see David Loye, "Kurt Lewin and the Black-and-White Sickness," *Psychology Today*, May, 1971, p. 74. For more extensive treatment of the subject see Arthur R. Cohen, *Attitude Change and Social Influence* (New York: Basic Books, 1964); Kurt Lewin, *Resolving Social Conflicts*, pp. 110-21; Leon Festinger, *A Theory of Cognitive Dissonance* (Stanford: Stanford University Press, 1957); Leon Festinger, Henry W. Riecken, and Stanley Schachter, *When Prophecy Fails* (Minneapolis: University of Minnesota Press, 1956).

16. The extent to which people tend to personalize bad news and blame the bearer or the injured party is explored in a fascinating book by William Ryan, *Blaming the Victim* (New York: Pantheon Books, 1971). While the book is directed at the subject of poverty, any advocate of planned change will find the last chapter to be very provocative on the general issue of America's approach to social change.

17. Michael J. Connor, "Maternity Homes See an Uncertain Future as Occupancy Shrinks," *Wall Street Journal*, May 3, 1971.
18. For a fascinating account of institutional lag and of how the obedience to tradition can thwart efforts at innovation, see Donald A. Schon, "The Blindness System," *The Public Interest*, Winter, 1970, pp. 25-38. This case study also offers strong support for the concept of vesting control of an organization in the clientele.
19. For an excellent brief account of the changes that are beginning to take place in the operation of maternity homes, see Prudence M. Rains, "Moral Reinstatement: The Characteristics of Maternity Homes," *American Behavioral Scientist*, November/December, 1970, pp. 219-36.
20. Charles F. Herman, "Crisis and Organizational Viability," *Administrative Service Quarterly*, June, 1963, pp. 61-82.
21. Russell R. Dynes, "Organizational Involvement and Changes in Community Structure in Disaster," *American Behavioral Scientist*, January/February, 1970, pp. 435-39. This volume also includes a useful annotated bibliography on studies of disasters.
22. For a list of seventy-one general propositions about the consequences of a disaster, see Allen H. Barton, *Communities in Disaster* (New York: Doubleday & Company, 1969).

# Chapter 3: The Process of Planned Change

1. For a brief, lucid introduction to force field analysis see Thomas R. Bennett, *The Leader and the Process of Change*, pp. 45-55. For an application of the same concepts from a businessman's perspective, see Arnold J. Judson, *A Manager's Guide to Making Changes* (New York: John Wiley & Sons, 1966).
2. Alvin Pitcher, "Two Cities—Two Churches," *The Chicago Theological Seminary Register*, May, 1967, pp. 4-5.
3. Kurt Lewin, "Frontiers in Group Dynamic," *Human Relations*, No. 1 (1947), p. 34.
4. Ronald Lippitt, Jeanne Watson, and Bruce Westley, *The Dynamics of Planned Change* (New York: Harcourt Brace Jovanovich, 1958), p. 130.
5. *Ibid.*, pp. 136-40.
6. Harvey Seifert and Howard J. Clinebell, Jr., *Personal Growth and Social Change* (Philadelphia: Westminster Press, 1969), pp. 83-93.
7. George M. Beal, Ross C. Blount, Ronald E. Powers, and W.

John Johnson, *Social Action and Interaction in Program Planning* (Ames, Iowa: Iowa State University Press, 1966), p. 6.

8. Marshall B. Clinard, *Slums and Community Development* (New York: The Free Press, 1970), pp. 283-85. See also Frank H. Sehnert, *A Functional Framework for the Action Process in Community Development* (Carbondale: Department of Community Development, Southern Illinois University, 1961), pp. 87-92; William W. Biddle, *The Community Development Process* (New York: Holt, Rinehart & Winston, 1965), pp. 90-102; James Q. Wilson, "An Overview of Theories of Planned Change," in Robert Morris, ed., *Centrally Planned Change* (New York: National Association of Social Workers, 1964), pp. 12-40; and Richard Flacks, "Strategies for Radical Social Change," *Social Policy*, March/April, 1971, pp. 7-14.

9. Christopher Sower, John Holland, Kenneth Tiedke, and Walter Freeman, *Community Involvement* (Glencoe: Free Press, 1958), pp. 306-14.

10. For a worldwide view of various causes and forms of discontent, see Bernard Crick and William A. Robson, eds., *Protest and Discontent* (Baltimore: Penguin Books, 1970).

11. For a recent description of this famous organizer's tactics, see Saul Alinsky, *Rules for Radicals* (New York: Random House, 1970), pp. 126-64; For an earlier analysis of his work, see Lyle E. Schaller, *Community Organization: Conflict and Reconciliation* (Nashville: Abingdon Press, 1966).

12. From an article by Pat Krochmal, "Language of Report by Walker Offensive," *Chicago Today*, May 22, 1969.

13. For an elaboration of this point, see Murray Ross, *Community Organization—Theory and Principles* (New York: Harper & Row, 1955), pp. 156-64.

14. An interesting, and at times amusing, illustration of how rhetoric can become a diversion from the issue, as well as cloud the distinctions between the reformer and the revolutionary, can be seen in an essay by Louis J. Halle, "The Student Drive to Destruction," *The New Republic*, October 19, 1968, and in the responses to this article and Halle's response to these letters in the November 23, 1968 issue.

15. William A. Ganson, *Power and Discontent* (Homewood, Ill.: The Dorsey Press, 1968), pp. 190-91.

16. For an elaboration of the vision and model concept, see Lyle E. Schaller, *Parish Planning*, pp. 79-81.

17. For an elaboration of this point, see *ibid.*, pp. 75-88.

18. For a more detailed description of the legislative problems encountered by the amendment, see Arlen J. Large, "Fallen

Women: An Amendment Fails," *The Wall Street Journal*, December 22, 1970.

19. Quoted in John Prestbo, "More Citizens Sue to Force Government to Stop or Start Acts," *Wall Street Journal*, April 16, 1971.

20. For a provocative attack on "interest-group liberalism" as an obsolete political philosophy that has undercut the concept of due process of law, see Theodore Lowi, *The End of Liberalism* (New York: W. W. Norton, 1969), p. 287. Lowi argues that in an era when human relations must be the number-one concern of government, the traditional liberal-conservative labels, which have been obsolete since 1937, and the elevation of interest-group pluralism from a theory to an ideology have obscured the real reasons for the current crisis of public authority. He contends that "the corruption of modern democratic government began with the emergence of interest-group liberalism as the public philosophy" and favors replacing interest-group liberalism with juridical democracy. For two excellent introductions to coalition politics, see Bayard Rustin, "Black Power and Coalition Politics," *Commentary*, September, 1966, and William H. Riker, *The Theory of Political Coalitions* (New Haven: Yale University Press, 1962).

21. Quoted in *Time*, April 11, 1969, p. 40. See also John W. Gardner, *Self-Renewal* (New York: Harper & Row, 1965).

22. Karl Hertz, "A Utopian Tract," *The Lutheran Quarterly*, XVIII, (1966), 26. For a fascinating case study of an effort to predict and influence social change, see *The Rise and Fall of Project Camelot*, ed. Irving Louis Horowitz (Cambridge, Mass.: The M.I.T. Press, 1967).

23. A review of the attack on the use of land use controls as a discriminatory device can be found in Paul Davidoff and Neil N. Gold, "Exclusionary Zoning," *Law and Social Action*, Winter, 1970, pp. 56-63.

24. *Campus Unrest*, The Report of the President's Commission on Campus Unrest (Washington: The United States Government Printing Office, 1970), pp. 117-47.

25. Fred W. Friendly, "The Unselling of the Selling of the Pentagon," *Harper's*, June, 1971, pp. 30-37.

26. The fireworks created when a strategy for change encounters the strategy for maintaining the status quo is described in Robert Lefcourt, ed., *Law Against the People* (New York: Random House, 1971). This is an attempt to demonstrate how the law tends to oppress the poor and other marginal groups and suggests some of the changes required if the judicial system is to be an effective vehicle for planned social change.

27. An outstanding presentation of the concept of the anticipatory leader can be found in Robert K. Greenleaf, "The Servant as Leader," *Journal of Current Issues*, Spring, 1971, pp. 2-29. In this excerpt from his book of the same title Greenleaf describes the "central ethic" of leadership as foresight, or the capability to look beyond today and to view one's own situation both from the perspective of the involved participant and from the detachment of the outsider. This concept of goal-centered leadership based on self-awareness and its importance to the process of planned change is described from another perspective by Warren Breed, *The Self-Guiding Society* (New York: The Free Press, 1971).

# Chapter 4: Questions for the Change Agent

1. It should not be assumed from this and other illustrations that the community-development approach is appropriate only for a rural economy. For an appraisal of the community-development corporation and its value in urban communities, and especially in impoverished black neighborhoods, see CDSs, *New Hope for the Inner City* (New York: The Twentieth Century Fund, 1971). This report vigorously encourages the creation of more community-development corporations. For an extraordinarily detailed, nontheoretical, and pragmatic handbook for organizers, see *The Organizer's Manual* (New York: Bantam Books, 1971). This small volume has an exceptionally complete bibliography. It also offers the over-thirty reader some remarkable insights into the radical activism of the 1970s.

2. Douglas McGregor, *The Human Side of Enterprise* (New York: McGraw-Hill, 1960).

3. For a brief biographical sketch of McGregor's life, and for some other examples of his thinking, see *Leadership and Motivation*, ed. Warren G. Bennis and Edgar H. Schein (Cambridge, Massachusetts: The M.I.T. Press, 1966).

4. *Ibid.*, p. 15.

5. Gerald J. Jud, "The Local Church and the Big Daddy Fantasy," *Crisis in the Church*, ed. Everett C. Parker (Philadelphia: Pilgrim Press, 1968), pp. 39-49.

6. Richard M. Levine, "The End of the Politics of Pleasure," and Jeremy Larner, "Jess Unruh and His Moment of Truth," *Harper's*, April, 1971.

7. For a sensitive discussion of the nature of a collaborative style

of leadership and the issue of manipulation and coercion, see Harvey Seifert and Howard J. Clinebell, Jr., *Personal Growth and Social Change*, pp. 52-59.

8. Roger Shinn, "The Locus of Authority: Participatory Democracy in the Age of the Expert," *Erosion of Authority*, ed. Clyde L. Manschreck (Nashville: Abingdon Press, 1971).

9. Quoted in Francis Pierce, "Welfare on the Cheap," *The New Republic*, February 22, 1969, p. 24.

10. For a detailed description of this rule change and its early consequences, see Norman C. Miller, "House Reform Begins to Take Hold," *Wall Street Journal*, April 2, 1971.

11. "St. Louis' Pruitt-Igoe Fate Hanging in Balance," *Journal of Housing*, April, 1971, pp. 190-91.

12. The degree to which alienation and depersonalization has become a major concern of public administrators is symbolized by the January/February, 1969 issue of *Public Administration Review*, which devoted one half of the issue to a symposium on that subject. Several provocative analyses of the destructive forces of social change can be found in John Paul Scott and Sarah F. Scott, eds., *Social Control and Social Change* (Chicago: The University of Chicago Press, 1971). A thoughtful and valuable description of the positive dimensions of disorder can be found in Theodore J. Lowi, *The Politics of Disorder* (New York: Basic Books, 1971). The three-page prologue offers an excellent frame of reference for those seeking to change obsolete institutions.

13. Harrison C. White, "Multipliers, Vacancy Chains, and Filtering in Housing," *Journal of the American Institute of Planners*, March, 1971, pp. 80-94.

14. Quoted in Jane Floerchinger, "Agricultural Revolution Is Social Disaster," *The Wichita Eagle*, June 2, 1971, p. 7A.

15. Theodore Levitt, *Innovation in Marketing* (New York: McGraw-Hill, 1962), pp. 74-75.

16. Steve Allen, "The Uses of Comedy," *The Center Magazine*, January/February, 1971, p. 19.

## Chapter 5: The Use of Power and Social Change

1. Robert A. Dahl, *A Preface to Democratic Theory* (Chicago: University of Chicago Press, 1956), pp. 12, 13, 31. For a remarkably perceptive and realistic analysis of the tactics of the change agent, see Christopher Lasch, "Can the Left Rise Again?"

*The New York Review of Books*, October 21, 1971, pp. 36-42. Lasch offers a very persuasive argument that a greater emphasis on the details of tactics will be more fruitful in changing "the system" than the sweeping historical synthesis or the broad socio-cultural analyses that are so popular with many living room advocates of change.

2. Herbert Simon, "Notes on the Observation and Measurement of Power," *Journal of Politics*, November, 1953, pp. 500-516.

3. Saul Alinsky, *Rules for Radicals* (New York: Random House, 1971), pp. 126-64.

4. Adolf A. Berle, *Power* (New York: Harcourt, Brace Jovanovich, 1969), pp. 39-58.

5. *Ibid.*, pp. 34-114.

6. Peter Bachrach and Morton S. Baratz, *Power and Poverty* (New York: Oxford University Press, 1970), pp. 3-16, 39-51.

7. John C. Bennett, "The Church and Power Conflicts," *Christianity and Crisis*, March 22, 1965, pp. 47-51.

8. Bachrach and Baratz, *Power and Poverty*, pp. 39-42.

9. Floyd Hunter, *Community Power Structure* (Chapel Hill: University of North Carolina Press, 1953).

10. The classic study is Robert A. Dahl, *Who Governs?* (New Haven: Yale University Press, 1961).

11. Robert M. MacIver, *Power Transformed* (New York: The Macmillan Co., 1964).

12. For an overview of the growing student protest movement, see John P. O'Brien, "The Development of the New Left" and the other essays in *The Annals of the American Academy of Political and Social Science*, May, 1971, pp. 15-25.

13. Howard D. Hamilton, "Direct Legislation: Some Duplications of Open Housing Referenda," *The American Political Science Review*, March, 1970, pp. 124-37.

14. For an exceptionally well-informed and lucid discussion of the problems of authority and democracy, see Robert A. Dahl, *After The Revolution?* (New Haven: Yale University Press, 1970).

15. For three substantially different analyses of this trend and its implications, see Max Ways, "More Power to Everybody," *Fortune*, May, 1970; Richard J. Barber, *The American Corporation* (New York: E. P. Dutton, 1970); and Lyle E. Schaller, *The Impact of the Future* (Nashville: Abingdon Press, 1969), pp. 196-203.

16. Sheldon J. Plager, "Policy, Planning and the Courts," *Journal of the American Institute of Planners*, May, 1971, pp. 174-91.

17. For one of the outstanding contemporary briefs on behalf of localism, or what the author refers to as "local liberty," see

Milton Kotler, *Neighborhood Government* (Indianapolis: Bobbs-Merrill, 1969). For a case study type of argument on the necessity of changing political structures in order to achieve social reform, see David Rogers, *The Management of Big Cities* (Beverly Hills, Calif.: Sage Publications, 1971). Rogers contends that a strategy for social change must stress better management rather than simply call for increasing the financial resources.

18. For three different approaches to this dilemma, see Paul Tillich, *Love, Power and Justice* (New York: Oxford University Press, 1960); Dieter T. Hessel, *Reconciliation and Conflict* (Philadelphia: Westminster Press, 1969); and Harvey Seifert and Howard J. Clinebell, *Personal Growth and Social Change*, pp. 191-219.

# Chapter 6: Anticipating and Managing Conflict

1. Norman C. Miller, "Who Are the Voters?" *Wall Street Journal*," November 5, 1968. For a more extensive and systematic analysis of this subject, see Richard M. Scammon and Ben J. Wattenberg, *Real Majority* (New York: Coward-McCann & Geoghegan, 1970).

2. *The Lutheran*, May 8, 1968, p. 25. For a more extensive analysis of Gallup Polls on religion, see George Gallup, Jr., and John O. Davies III, eds., *Religion in America*, 1971 (Princeton: Gallup International, Inc., 1971).

3. Robert A. Dahl, *After the Revolution?* pp. 3-58.

4. Roger L. Shinn, "The Locus of Authority: Participatory Democracy in the Age of the Expert," pp. 92-122. For a good introduction to the establishment of legitimate authority, see Charles F. Andrain, *Political Life and Social Change* (Belmont, Calif.: Wadsworth Publishing Company, 1970), pp. 129-47.

5. For a recent outstanding effort to use the budget as a means of resolving conflict, in this case a response by the National Urban Coalition to the conflict over national priorities, see *Counterbudget*, ed. Robert S. Benson and Harold Wolman (New York: Praeger, 1971).

6. For a distinction between game theory and games on simulation see Harold Guetzkow, et al., *Simulation in International Relations: Developments for Research and Teaching* (Englewood Cliffs, N. J.: Prentice-Hall, 1963), pp. 211-12. For a lucid introduction to simulation, see William A. Ganson, ed, *Simsoc* (New York: The Free Press, 1969). For a slightly more advanced introduction to scientific gaming, see John R. Rader,

*Simulation and Society* (Boston: Allyn and Bacon, 1969). An excellent nontechnical introduction is Morton D. Davis, *Game Theory* (New York: Basic Books, 1970). A useful review article on gaming is Martin Patchen, "Models of Cooperation and Conflict: A Critical Review," *The Journal of Conflict Resolution,* September, 1970, pp. 389-407. Another excellent introduction to the subject is Michael Inbar and Clarice S. Stoll, eds., *Simulation and Gaming in Social Science* (New York: The Free Press, 1971).

7. Rolf Dahrendorf, *Class and Class Conflict in Industrial Society* (Stanford: Stanford University Press, 1959), p. 234. For an illustration of how tactical mistakes can unnecessarily intensify conflict in an organization, see Harold R. Fray, Jr., *Conflict and Change in the Church* (Philadelphia: Pilgrim Press, 1969), p. 47. This book is an outstanding account of how a congregation learned to live with conflict.

8. Lewis Coser, *The Functions of Social Conflict* (New York: The Free Press, 1956). Arthur I. Waskow, *From Race Riot to Sit-In* (Garden City, N. Y.: Doubleday & Company, 1966), pp. 203-4. Marcus Borg, *Conflict and Social Change* (Minneapolis: Augsburg Publishing House, 1971), pp. 70-76.

9. For an excellent discussion of the creative management of conflict, see Harvey Seifert and Howard J. Clinebell, *Personal Growth and Social Change,* pp. 163-70.

10. James S. Coleman, *Community Conflict* (New York: The Free Press, 1957), p. 8.

## Chapter 7: Organizational Change

1. Arthur M. Schlesinger, Jr., *A Thousand Days* (Boston: Houghton Mifflin, 1965), pp. 407-47.

2. Theodore C. Sorenson, *Kennedy* (New York: Harper & Row, 1965), pp. 287-90.

3. For a more recent description of how the influence of the State Department has diminished as the agency has grown in size, see John Franklin Campbell, *The Foreign Affairs Fudge Factory* (New York: Basic Books, 1971). For an analysis of large organizations and the impact on the people who work in them, see Robert Presthus, *The Organizational Society* (New York: Random House, 1962).

4. Campbell, *The Foreign Affairs Fudge Factory.* The importance of working for change in organizations has gained considerable

attention in recent years from a variety of scholars. In his pioneering study, *Linkage Politics* (New York: The Free Press, 1969), James N. Rosenau pointed out how what happens within one organization has far-reaching implications that are felt in remote places. While he wrote from a different perspective, Reinhold Niebuhr had as much to say to the student of organization development as any theologian. For a brief but lucid review of the impact on Niebuhr's pessimism about the possibility of reforming social institutions, see William A. Clebsch, *From Sacred to Profane America* (New York: Harper & Row, 1968), pp. 171-74.

5. More recently a number of other terms have emerged to describe what Drucker called "the new reality." This list includes Drucker's "The Age of Discontinuity," and Michael Harrington's "The Accidental Century"; Margaret Mead's concept of persons born before 1945 as immigrants to a new era; Zbigniew Brzezinski's "Technetronic Era"; Alvin Toffler's "Super-Industrial Revolution"; Bertram M. Gross's "Service Society"; Kenneth Boulding's "Post-Civilization"; and Charles Reich's "Consciousness III."

6. For a lucid and concise definition of the term see Warren G. Bennis, *Organization Development: Its Nature, Origins and Prospects* (Reading, Mass.: Addison-Wesley Publishing Co., 1968). For a more extensive discussion of organizational revitalization, see Warren G. Bennis, *Changing Organizations* (New York: McGraw-Hill, 1966).

7. Samuel Lubell, *The Hidden Crisis in American Politics* (New York: W. W. Norton, 1970).

8. For another analysis of the conditions which created the need for organization development, see Warren G. Bennis and Philip E. Slater, *The Temporary Society* (New York: Harper & Row, 1968), pp. 53-76. This was one of the most influential essays on leadership to be published during the 1960s.

9. Richard Beckhard, *Organization-Development: Strategies and Models* (Reading, Mass.: Addison-Wesley Publishing Co., 1968), pp. 9-14.

10. John W. Gardner, *Self-Renewal.*

11. Adapted from a definition of process consultation in Edgar Schein, *Process Consultation: Its Role in Organization Development* (Reading, Mass.: Addison-Wesley Publishing Co., 1969), pp. 8-9.

12. From the 1969 Report of the Board of Christian Education to the 95th General Assembly of the Presbyterian Church in Canada. For a brief but very useful statement on the local church

in organizational terms, see Robert C. Worley, *Change in the Church: A Source of Hope* (Philadelphia: Westminster Press, 1971), pp. 96-127. For a specific denominational approach, see Elaine Dickson, "Theory and Process of Change for Southern Baptists," *Search*, Fall, 1970, pp. 23-28.

13. For an elaboration of this strategy, see Beckhard, *Organization Development: Strategies and Models*, pp. 27-33.

14. For an elaboration of this strategy, see R. R. Blake, H. A. Shepart, and J. S. Mouton, *Managing Intergroup Conflict in Industry* (Houston: Gulf Publishing Co. 1965).

15. Schein, *Process Consultation: Its Role in Organization Development*, pp. 15-30.

16. Chris Argyris, "Understanding Human Behavior in Organizations: One Viewpoint," *Modern Organization Theory*, ed. Mason Harre (New York: John Wiley & Sons, 1959), pp. 115-54. For an excellent introduction to organizational change in voluntary associations, see Ray Johns, *Confronting Organizational Change* (New York: Association Press, 1963).

17. This point is made most forcefully by Frances Fox Piven and Richard A. Cloward, *Regulating the Poor* (New York: Pantheon Books, 1971). The authors contend that welfare is not primarily charity or for the relief of the poor, but is primarily a system for regulating the poor. Anyone seeking to change the welfare system must recognize that relief is only a secondary function of the welfare system. For another very significant analysis of the impact of the poverty subculture, see Herbert Hirsch, *Poverty and Politicization* (New York: The Free Press, 1971). His application of social learning theory merits the careful scrutiny of anyone interested in organization development.

18. The details are described by Burt Schorr, "Government Reorganization: Tough Going," *Wall Street Journal*, March 26, 1971.

19. For an elaboration of this, see Harvey Wheeler, "The Politics of Revolution," *The Center Magazine*, March, 1968.

20. A more extensive account can be found in Wallace Roberts, "Can Urban Schools Be Reformed?" *The Saturday Review*, May 17, 1969, pp. 70-91. For a more penetrating analysis of the need for change in public schools and a provocative response, see Ivan Illich, *Deschooling Society* (New York: Harper & Row, 1971).

# Index